The Ministry of Money

The Ministry of Money
A Treasurer's Role in the Mission of the Church

© 2025 Keith Clark-Hoyos
All rights reserved.

No part of this publication may be reproduced, stored in a retrieval system, or transmitted in any form or by any means—electronic, mechanical, photocopying, recording, or otherwise—without the prior written permission of the author,
except in the case of brief quotations embodied in critical articles or reviews.

Published by Clark-Hoyos Publishing
ISBN: 979-8-9987673-4-0

Library of Congress Control Number: [Pending]

Cover and interior design by Keith Clark-Hoyos

Printed in the United States of America

For permissions or bulk orders, contact:
Church Training Center
community.churchtrainingcenter.com

Permissions Notice

Scripture quotations marked (NIV) are from the *Holy Bible, New International Version®, NIV®*, Copyright © 1973, 1978, 1984, 2011 by Biblica, Inc.® Used by permission. All rights reserved worldwide.

Scripture quotations marked (NRSV) are from the *New Revised Standard Version Bible*, copyright © 1989 National Council of the Churches of Christ in the United States of America. Used by permission. All rights reserved.

Scripture quotations marked (NRSVUE) are from the *New Revised Standard Version, Updated Edition*, Copyright © 2021 National Council of the Churches of Christ in the United States of America. Used by permission. All rights reserved.

Scripture quotations marked (ESV) are from *The Holy Bible, English Standard Version® (ESV®)*, copyright © 2001 by Crossway, a publishing ministry of Good News Publishers. Used by permission. All rights reserved.

Scripture quotations marked (CEB) are from the *Common English Bible*, copyright © 2011 by Common English Bible. Used by permission. All rights reserved.

The Ministry of Money

A Treasurer's Role in the Mission of the Church

Keith Clark-Hoyos

For every quiet steward who ever asked, "How does this budget reflect our faith?"
May your spreadsheets become prayers,
Your balance sheets become testimonies,
And your service bear witness to God's abundance.

Acknowledgments

With deep gratitude…

To the congregations who welcomed me into their stories—thank you for trusting me with your questions, your spreadsheets, and your sacred calling.

To the Church Training Center team, who helped carry the vision of this work with dedication, skill, and Spirit-led clarity.

To the Effective Church Leadership Community, whose faithfulness, feedback, and longing for integrity in ministry shaped every chapter of this book.

To my mentors and spiritual companions—both seen and unseen—who have formed me into the steward, teacher, and listener I strive to be.

To my beloved wife, **Zulima**—thank you for your unwavering love, your prayers behind the scenes, and your quiet strength in every season. This work is possible because of your support and faith in me.

And to Spirit,
Who still calls in whispers, nudges in silence, and provides more than I know how to ask.
May this offering bring clarity, courage, and blessing to all who receive it.

About the Author

Keith Clark-Hoyos is a dedicated leader known for his unwavering positivity and remarkable ability to guide and inspire within the realm of church leadership and administration. His life journey has been characterized by a deep commitment to personal and professional growth, a passion for teaching and coaching, and a profound love for nurturing individuals and organizations toward their highest potential.

In 2015, Keith transitioned from his role as a church judicatory leader to found Church Training Center — a thriving consulting, coaching, training, and accounting firm serving churches and nonprofits across the nation. Together with his wife and partner, he has built a team that supports mission-driven ministries with clarity, care, and Spirit-led wisdom.

Keith holds a Master of Arts in Ministry, Leadership & Service from Claremont School of Theology and an undergraduate degree in Business Administration and Church Ministries from Simpson University. He is also a Daoist Monk in the Wù Zhēn Pài (Awakened Reality Sect) lineage and brings a deeply contemplative and spiritually grounded presence to his work.

At the heart of Keith's calling is a desire to empower church leaders to live faithfully, lead effectively, and align all resources — financial, human, and spiritual — with the mission God has placed before them.

Table of Contents

Section	Page Number
How To Use This Resource	1
Preface	4
Part I: A Calling Entrusted	8
Chapter 1: Called to Diligence	10
Chapter 2: Faithful Stewards	22
Chapter 3: Guard the Deposit	34
Part II: Systems That Safeguard	46
Chapter 4: Prudent Leadership	48
Chapter 5: Much Is Required	58
Chapter 6: Honor the Lord	64
Part III: Telling the Truth in Numbers	74
Chapter 7: Serve God Alone	76
Chapter 8: Truth in the Inward Being	84
Chapter 9: Faithful Servants	92
Chapter 10: Sustaining Mission	98
Part IV: Budgets That Bear Witness	104
Chapter 11: Cheerful Givers	106
Chapter 12: Not In Vain	114
Chapter 13: Estimate The Cost	122
Part V: Serving Faithfully to the End	130
Chapter 14: What You Owe	132
Chapter 15: Silence The Ignorant	138
Chapter 16: What Is Right	144
Chapter 17: Keep The Faith	152
Epilogue	160
Appendix A: Scripture References	167
Appendix B: Key Terms Glossary	171
Appendix C: Treasurer's Annual Checklist	173
Index	175
Effective Church Leadership Community	178

How to Use This Resource

The Ministry of Money: A Treasurer's Role in the Mission of the Church is a guide for church treasurers, board members, clergy, and finance committees seeking to transform financial stewardship into a sacred calling. This section outlines how to engage with the book and its resources to align your congregation's finances with its mission.

Purpose and Audience

This book equips church leaders to manage finances with integrity, transparency, and spiritual discernment. Whether you're a new treasurer navigating budgets, a board member ensuring accountability, or a pastor aligning mission with money, these pages offer practical tools and theological insights to serve faithfully.

Structure

The book comprises 17 chapters, each structured to blend lived experience, scripture, and actionable steps:

Introduction: Grounds the theme in real-world challenges.

Theological Framing: Reflects on scripture to root financial practices in faith.

Practical Application: Provides tools, examples, and strategies, often linked to the Effective Church Leadership Community (ECLC).

Conclusion and Reflection Questions: Offers five questions for individual or group discernment.

Appendices provide scripture references, a glossary, and a treasurer's checklist, while the back matter links to additional resources.

Accessing the ECLC Library — Free with This Book

All tools, templates, and webinars referenced throughout the book—such as the **Financial Dashboard Template, Sample Financial Transparency Policy**, and the **Good Governance** webinar—are hosted in the **Effective Church Leadership Community (ECLC)**.

Access to ECLC is free with the purchase of this book. Scan the QR code in the back of the book to unlock the full library of resources.

Using the Book

- **Individual Study**: Read chapters sequentially or select those relevant to your role (e.g., Chapter 13 for cash flow). Use reflection questions to deepen personal discernment.
- **Group Study**: Facilitate finance committee or board workshops using reflection questions and *The Heart of Stewardship, The Practice of Faith*, a companion workbook available in the ECLC. Host budget forums or training sessions, as modeled in Chapter 12.
- **Practical Application**: Implement tools like the Financial Policies & Procedures Template or Sample Financial Transparency Policy to enhance accountability.

Getting Started

Begin with the **Preface** to understand the book's vision. For treasurers, start with **Chapter 1** to reframe your role as spiritual leadership. Boards may prioritize **Chapter 2** for fiduciary duty or **Chapter 15** for governance. Use *The Heart of Stewardship* for group exercises. Let this book be a companion in your journey to faithful stewardship—**supported by a growing library of free resources through the ECLC.**

Preface

It began with a shoebox.

Not a metaphor, not a tidy story—just a literal shoebox filled with folded receipts, scribbled notes, and unopened statements. The church treasurer, newly elected and completely overwhelmed, had been handed "the books" with a nervous laugh and the assurance that "God will help you figure it out." And in time, God did. But not without prayer, panic, and a crash course in faithful stewardship.

That story is not unique. Across the country, faithful leaders step into the role of church treasurer with willing hearts and little preparation. Some inherit QuickBooks files with no chart of accounts. Others are told that last year's budget will do fine again. Still others walk into boardrooms where mission is whispered and money shouted—where financial strain eclipses spiritual vision.

The Ministry of Money is for them. It is for the treasurer staring at a balance sheet that doesn't balance.

Each year, more money is stolen from churches than is spent on global missions. Fraud often hides in plain sight, unreported in 95% of nonprofit cases. Churches are especially vulnerable because of the very thing that makes them beautiful—a culture of trust. But treasurers are not just stewards of funds; they are guardians of that trust, protecting the witness of the church through integrity and diligence.

For the board chair wondering how to lead a conversation about payroll when giving is down. For the pastor wrestling with the gap between the gospel proclaimed and the budget approved. It is for all who sense that money, too, can be holy ground—if only we would walk it with wisdom and care.

This book is not just a manual. It is a map.

Structured across seventeen chapters, *The Ministry of Money* unfolds in four parts within each chapter: an Introduction that grounds the theme in lived experience, a Theological Framing that reflects on scripture and spiritual purpose, a Practical Application that outlines clear steps and examples, and a Conclusion and Reflection Questions that invite personal discernment. Each chapter closes with five questions designed for individual or group engagement. The book also includes Appendix A, listing all scripture references, and optional appendices for terminology and supporting tools if your congregation chooses to explore them.

This is a guide for treasurers—but not only for treasurers. It is for board members who want to serve with faith and clarity. It is for clergy who want to align their pastoral and financial leadership. It is for finance committees who yearn for their work to feel more like ministry and less like maintenance. At its core, this is a book about mission-driven financial leadership—about how we honor God in the way we steward every dollar, policy, and decision.

We live in a time where trust must be earned. Many churches are navigating complex terrain: shifting attendance, aging facilities, evolving giving patterns, legal compliance, and leadership transitions. It is not enough to balance a budget. Churches must also bear witness—to a gospel of transparency, integrity, generosity, and hope. The treasurer's role is not ancillary to this witness; it is essential.

And yet, the treasurer need not carry this alone. Throughout the book, you'll encounter stories of congregations who found their way through financial confusion—some slowly, some boldly, some with tears and laughter alike. What united them was not technical perfection, but a shared willingness to see their finances as part of their faith.

In Romans 12:8, Paul offers this charge: "…if it is leadership, let them govern diligently." Diligence, in this context, is more than work ethic. It is devotion. It is stewardship. It is the quiet faithfulness that shows up at month's end, ledger open, questions ready, heart listening. When treasurers govern with diligence, the church becomes more than sustainable—it becomes trustworthy.

As you begin this journey, bring your questions, your fears, your hopes. You do not need to be an accountant to lead well. What you need is a willingness to learn, a heart attuned to God's purpose, and a vision of money not as a burden, but as a tool for mission.

My prayer is that this book will offer clarity, courage, and companionship. That each chapter will feel like a conversation—honest, practical, grounded in Spirit. And that by the end, you will see your role not just as necessary, but sacred.

Welcome to the ministry of money.

Part I

A Calling Entrusted

Whatever you do, work at it with all your heart, as working for the Lord…
— Colossians 3:23

Chapter 1:
Do It Diligently;
Do It Cheerfully!

Reframing the Treasurer's Work as Spiritual Leadership

if it is to lead, do it diligently; if it is to show mercy, do it cheerfully
– Romans 12:8 (NIV)

Introduction

Church treasurers rarely seek the spotlight. Their names may not appear in the bulletin. They may not speak from the pulpit. Yet their work speaks volumes — not only about the financial condition of the church, but about the integrity, health, and spiritual direction of the entire body. In many churches, the treasurer is one of the only people who consistently sees the whole picture — the rhythms of giving, the gaps between intention and action, the alignment (or misalignment) between Calling and resources.

And yet, most treasurers aren't trained for this. They come to the role through trust, not through theological or financial credentials. They may carry uncertainty, feel isolated, or worry that they are "just the bookkeeper." But let this chapter begin with a truth that will shape everything that follows:

A treasurer is not just a financial officer — they are a **spiritual leader**. Their work is a ministry. Their voice matters.

In *Embracing Our Call*, we describe leadership as a spiritual discipline rooted in discernment — a call to listen, not control. That principle applies deeply here. The church treasurer must not only keep accurate records, but **read the signs**. They are often the first to notice what isn't being said — trends in giving, quiet shifts in expenses, or areas of ministry that are being underfunded despite public support. These observations aren't just administrative. They are invitations to **pause, pray, and realign**.

That's why Romans 12:8 is such a fitting foundation: *"if it is to lead, do it diligently; if it is to show mercy, do it cheerfully"* (NIV). Diligence and cheerfulness may seem like small things — but in the life of a treasurer, they are everything. They point to a way of serving that is both exacting and joyful, detailed and Spirit-filled.

The treasurer, by nature of the role, is entrusted with great responsibility. In *Serving the Call*, we refer to this as **sacred responsibility** — the idea that leadership is not merely a task list, but a covenant. The treasurer's covenant is this: to ensure the financial story of the church reflects the **spiritual story God is writing through the church.**

This begins with posture. Treasurers who approach their work as a sacred trust bring a different tone to the table. They are not driven by fear or scarcity, but by **purpose and clarity.** They understand that the budget is not just a spreadsheet — it's a **spiritual map**, showing what the church values, who it's serving, and whether its actions align with its professed Calling.

But let's be honest: many treasurers don't feel this way when they start. They may be carrying the pressure of monthly reports, facing conflicting expectations, or wondering whether anyone really listens. They may feel like the "finance person" in a ministry team full of pastors, teachers, and visionaries. This is where the discernment framework from *Called Together* offers a needed shift. In that guide, discernment begins with noticing — observing what is, with clarity and compassion. Treasurers are often the **first ones to notice** when a financial pattern signals a deeper need, misalignment, or opportunity.

That's the heart of the role. Treasurers are **mission interpreters**. Their reports do more than present facts — they offer insight. Through diligence and cheerfulness, they invite the church to see the story being told through its money. Are we living what we claim to believe? Are our budgets aligned with our Calling? Is the Spirit leading us toward something more?

The treasurer is not alone in answering these questions. But they are often the one who **names them first** — and that's a sacred act of leadership. When the treasurer says, "Let's take a closer look," or "This number surprised me," they are not just flagging a detail.

They are opening space for reflection. That is the quiet power of this ministry: not to make every decision, but to hold the mirror with care.

In the sections that follow, we will explore the theological framing of this role, offer real-world tools and a powerful true story, and close with reflection questions that can guide any treasurer — new or seasoned — into a deeper sense of Calling.

You are not "just the treasurer." You are a **discernment leader**, a **financial shepherd**, and a **mission interpreter**.

Your work is spiritual.
Your diligence is devotion.
Your cheerfulness is witness.

Theological Framing

The treasurer's role is often assumed to be technical — numbers, spreadsheets, balances, reports. But within a spiritually aligned church, the treasurer is far more than a recordkeeper. They are, in truth, a **mission interpreter** — a spiritual leader who listens for God's movement through financial realities and helps the church discern whether its actions match its Calling.

In *Embracing Our Call*, the foundation of spiritual leadership is laid clearly: **we listen before we lead**. The treasurer's work embodies this. They listen to the numbers. They listen to the trends. And they listen to the Spirit's whisper within the tension between what is and what is called to be. Before they advise, before they present, before they recommend, they must first **discern**.

This mirrors the larger pattern in Romans 12:8 — *"if it is to lead, do it diligently; if it is to show mercy, do it cheerfully"* (NIV). Diligence and cheerfulness are not just character traits. They are theological postures. Diligence reflects faithfulness. Cheerfulness reflects grace. A treasurer who is both diligent and cheerful is not just good at the job — they are living into **a spiritual vocation**.

In the "Mission, Vision & Values" webinar (at 15:30), we examine how a church's spiritual identity must guide every structural and financial decision. One slide asks plainly: *"What is the bottom line in the Church?"* The answer isn't income or surplus. It's Calling. If our budgets don't reflect our Calling, then even a balanced spreadsheet can be a sign of spiritual misalignment. The treasurer is the first to see this — and the one most equipped to name it.

This is what it means to **steward the Calling**. Not to protect old patterns, but to remain rooted in God's purpose. Acts 4:34 describes the early church: *"There were no needy persons among them."* Why? Because they were aligned. Their spiritual convictions and financial practices were in sync. That's the kind of integrity the treasurer is entrusted to help maintain — not through control, but through clarity.

Clarity, however, is not always easy. Church budgets often carry decades of assumptions, staff requests, legacy expenses, and old narratives about scarcity or obligation. When a treasurer steps into this system, they may feel pressure to "just make it work" or to avoid rocking the boat. But spiritual leadership doesn't mean playing it safe — it means leading the church toward **alignment with the Spirit**.

That may mean gently asking:

"Why are we spending so much on this program?"

"Does this reflect our current sense of Calling?"

"Is this budget helping us love our neighbors more clearly?"

These are not critical questions — they are **courageous ones**. And they must be asked with the kind of pastoral posture modeled in

Serving the Call — clarity without condemnation, purpose without pressure.

In the "Why * Be * Do" webinar, we hear the three-part structure of faithful leadership: **Who we are, who we are called to be, and what we are called to do.** The treasurer's work engages all three:

> **BE** — by remaining rooted in their own sense of calling to this role
>
> **WHY** — by holding the mission clearly and calling the church back to it
>
> **DO** — by aligning budgets, processes, and decisions with that Calling
>
> This is a spiritual act — not a mechanical one.

When the treasurer stands before the board with a report, they are not just delivering data — they are delivering an invitation to reflect. That's why cheerfulness matters. Not because the work is easy, but because joy is a sign of trust. A treasurer who carries the work with joy invites others to see it as good and holy — even when it's hard.

Diligence without joy becomes duty.
Joy without diligence becomes denial.
But diligence *with* cheerfulness — that's where spiritual leadership lives.

The treasurer does not lead alone. But their voice is essential. They are the mirror-holders, the story-revealers, the ones who say, *"Here is what's true. Now, what shall we do?"*

This is why the treasurer must be trained not just in accounting, but in **discernment**. Not just in compliance, but in **calling**.

And this is why the next section — grounded in a real story — will show what happens when a treasurer speaks from that place of clarity.

Practical Application

Several years ago, I worked with a small rural church that operated a weekday outreach ministry supported in part by government funds. Reviewing the monthly financial statements, I noticed something that didn't add up: government reimbursements were higher than anticipated, but "participant support" revenue—the line designated for client contributions—was significantly lower than budgeted.

When I asked the treasurer about the discrepancy, she paused, then smiled. "We expected a certain number of clients would pay a sliding fee," she explained. "But more families qualified for full reimbursement than we projected. It turns out we're serving more people with greater financial need than we anticipated—about 20% more than we budgeted for."

What might have seemed like a deficit on one line was, in fact, evidence of a deeper truth: the ministry was working. The church's presence in the community was meeting a real and growing need. The treasurer didn't just explain the variance—she interpreted the mission. That moment shifted the conversation. Her quiet interpretation of the numbers reframed the financial report as a testimony of God's provision and the church's faithfulness.

This is the essence of what it means to be a **mission interpreter**. A treasurer is not merely the one who tracks what was spent and what was received. The treasurer reads the signs, discerns the patterns, and helps the board see what the Spirit might be revealing in the life of the congregation.

Financial tools such as budgets, reports, and audits are not just for compliance—they are instruments of clarity. They can tell us when we are off course, but also when we are faithfully following God's call, even if the numbers don't look the way we expected.

The treasurer's ministry is to listen deeply, to lead faithfully, and to ensure that decisions about money reflect discernment about mission. As you move through this book, that principle will guide each chapter: the treasurer as a spiritual leader—called not only to manage the money, but to reveal its meaning.

Conclusion and Reflection Questions

You may not have asked for this role. Many treasurers are elected, appointed, or encouraged into the work with little preparation and less ceremony. But you are here. And this work — as invisible, quiet, or misunderstood as it may feel — is sacred.

You are a keeper of truth.
You are a weaver of clarity.
You are the one who helps the church see what it cannot see on its own.

The treasurer is the mission interpreter — not because they speak for God, but because they ask *faithful questions* in a language the church often forgets it can understand. Numbers are not the opposite of spirituality. In the hands of a spiritually grounded treasurer, they are **a mirror held up to the soul of the church**.

Romans 12:8 says, *"if it is to lead, do it diligently; if it is to show mercy, do it cheerfully"* (NIV). This charge is not about personality. It's about posture. It reminds us that diligence is not just about getting the job done. It is about being faithful to what matters most — protecting the integrity of the church's financial witness, aligning money with mission, and speaking truth without fear.

Cheerfulness is not denial. It is **evidence of grace** — a way of carrying the work without bitterness, trusting that God is in it with you.

In *Serving the Call*, the theme of sacred responsibility is woven throughout every chapter. This is your sacred responsibility: to tend the financial life of the church with joy, humility, and courage. When you do this work with diligence and cheerfulness, you are living the very definition of spiritual leadership.

As this chapter comes to a close, let its purpose remain simple and strong:

You are not just the treasurer.
You are a **discernment leader**.
You are a **truth-teller**.
You are a **servant of the mission**.

And you are not alone.

There is a community of church leaders walking this path with you. The **Effective Church Leadership Community** exists to equip you with the tools, reflection guides, and encouragement you need. Whether it's using the Clarity Worksheet Template to lead your board through discernment, or opening your meetings with prayerful silence, or reminding your team that financial reports are spiritual documents — your work matters.

And not just to the budget.
Not just to the board.
It matters to the body of Christ.

Because when you help the church walk in financial integrity, you help it walk in spiritual freedom.

🕊 Reflection Questions

1. How does Romans 12:8 inspire your role in serving the church with diligence and faith?
2. In what ways have you acted as a "mission interpreter" when reviewing financial data or sharing reports?
3. Describe a moment when a financial variance revealed something deeper about your church's ministry. What did it teach you?
4. How can your church's budget and reports reflect both spiritual faithfulness and practical clarity?
5. What practices could help you listen more deeply to what the Spirit might be revealing through the church's financial story?

Chapter 2:

Prove Faithful

Fiduciary Duty and the
Sacred Work of
Accountability

*Now it is required that those who have been given a
trust must prove faithful*
– 1 Corinthians 4:2 (NIV)

Introduction

In every generation, God entrusts the work of ministry to people — not just pastors or preachers, but stewards. Those who are given the tools, resources, and responsibilities to hold space for the mission. Among them stands the treasurer, quietly managing what has been given in trust. That word — *trust* — is not a formality. It's a sacred framing.

Paul writes in 1 Corinthians 4:2, *"Now it is required that those who have been given a trust must prove faithful"* (NIV). This is the essence of fiduciary duty: not just legal compliance, but **spiritual accountability**. To be entrusted with something holy — and to remain faithful in how we manage it.

In *Embracing Our Call*, the chapter on "Stewardship as Ministry" reminds us that faithfulness is not defined by control, but by alignment. We are not called to manage outcomes, but to ensure that what we hold — time, energy, money, people — is used in a way that reflects God's purpose. That is the heart of fiduciary duty. It is **not a financial term** — it is a **discipleship term**.

Too often, church boards misunderstand fiduciary duty as guarding against risk or catching fraud. Those are pieces of the picture, yes — but the deeper call is this: **Are we stewarding what God has given in a way that proves faithful?**

This chapter explores the sacred work of accountability. Not the punitive kind, but the kind that says, *"Because we have been trusted with much, we must handle it with care, with transparency, and with truth."* In the "Good Governance" webinar, we're reminded that every board member — and especially those with financial oversight — is bound by three duties: care, loyalty, and obedience. These aren't just legal markers. They are spiritual ones.

The **Duty of Care** calls treasurers to act with wisdom, prudence, and attentiveness — not just doing the minimum, but attending faithfully to the needs of the church.

The **Duty of Loyalty** invites treasurers to put the mission above ego, politics, or personal preferences — choosing the church's Calling over convenience.

The **Duty of Obedience** centers everything on alignment with the church's purpose — returning again and again to the question: *Are we being who God has called us to be?*

When seen this way, fiduciary duty is not a burden — it's a **sacred trust**.

But treasurers are often caught between two worlds. On one side are legal obligations, policy documents, and accounting principles. On the other are spiritual values, congregational expectations, and pastoral dynamics. Navigating both requires more than technical skill — it requires **discernment**.

In *Called Together*, discernment is framed as faithful listening — not rushing to act, but pausing to reflect. Treasurers embody this when they ask:

"Is this budget aligned with our Calling?"

"Is this expenditure furthering our mission?"

"Are we building systems of trust, or just following rules?"

These are not questions of compliance — they are questions of **faithfulness**.

At times, accountability will mean asking hard questions. At other times, it will mean resisting the urge to speak first — and instead creating space for deeper reflection. But always, it means being willing to hold up a mirror to the church's financial practices and ask, *"Does this reflect who we believe we are?"*

That is the work of the treasurer. That is the path of proving faithful.

Theological Framing

To be entrusted with the church's finances is to hold something holy. Not just because of the dollars involved, but because of what those dollars represent: the prayers of givers, the work of ministry, and the future of the congregation. Fiduciary duty, then, is not a technical box to check — it is a **spiritual covenant**. A commitment to walk with integrity, to listen for God's direction, and to make decisions that reflect more than prudence — they reflect **faithfulness**.

In *Embracing Our Call*, the concept of "Stewardship as Ministry" is clear: when we manage church resources, we are doing more than balancing a budget. We are tending to the life of the church. This means our accountability isn't just to the board or the IRS — it's to God. It's to the Calling we have received. This is what 1 Corinthians 4:2 points us toward: *"Now it is required that those who have been given a trust must prove faithful"* (NIV). Not successful. Not impressive. But faithful.

That distinction matters.

In the "Good Governance" webinar (around slide 14), we see the duties of board members laid out clearly: care, loyalty, and obedience. These aren't merely legal constructs — they are *discipleship practices*.

> **Care** reminds us that our actions should always come from attentiveness, wisdom, and love — not apathy or neglect.

Loyalty challenges us to serve the church's mission, not our own preferences or affiliations.

Obedience calls us to align our financial leadership with the church's God-given purpose.

When lived out together, these duties create a framework for leadership that is both **legally sound and spiritually grounded**.

That's the treasurer's space. Not just at the spreadsheet or the board table, but at the intersection where mission meets money. Where a policy question becomes a discernment moment. Where the numbers invite us to ask: *Are we aligned with our Calling, or have we drifted into comfort, habit, or self-protection?*

This is why the treasurer must lead with integrity. Because trust isn't automatic — it is built, line by line, report by report, conversation by conversation. And in congregational settings, trust is easily broken. When financial decisions are hidden, rushed, or unexplained, people become suspicious. But when the treasurer offers clarity, transparency, and openness — trust grows. And with it, **spiritual maturity**.

In *Serving the Call*, trust is presented not as a vague feeling, but as a measurable outcome of clear roles, fair processes, and shared accountability. Treasurers contribute to this deeply. When you hold the line on reporting standards, when you raise concerns with grace, when you bring difficult truths into the light gently but clearly — you are **discipling the church in integrity**.

Accountability, in this context, is not punitive. It is restorative. It is what allows the church to remain focused, humble, and aligned. When the treasurer holds financial reports up to the light and asks, *"Are we being faithful with what we've been given?"* — they are protecting the mission. Not guarding it with fear, but **stewarding it with wisdom**.

This is what we mean when we say the treasurer's work is sacred. The numbers matter, yes. But what they **mean** matters even more. They tell the story of who we are — and who we are becoming.

And that is why fiduciary duty — when rooted in theology — becomes a gift. A calling. A spiritual practice.

The next section will explore what this looks like in practice: from transparency policies to trust-building strategies, and how the treasurer's role creates conditions for integrity and clarity across the church.

When treasurers embody fiduciary responsibility as a sacred trust, they shift the culture of the church. Accountability no longer feels like suspicion or bureaucracy. It becomes part of the church's witness — the way it shows the world that it can be trusted, that it operates with clarity, and that its mission is more than words on a page.

That shift happens not just in philosophy, but in practice. And the treasurer often leads the way.

One essential step in building a culture of trust is implementing clear, transparent financial reporting. The Sample Financial Transparency Policy, available in the Effective Church Leadership Community (ECLC), outlines core practices every treasurer can adopt. These include: • Regular reporting to the board and congregation • Explaining reports in plain language, not just technical terms • Making year-to-date and budget comparison data available to leaders • Establishing clear processes for reviewing and approving large expenditures

These practices aren't just procedural — they are pastoral. They allow church members to feel included, informed, and respected. And they prevent confusion or secrecy from damaging the church's credibility.

In one mid-sized congregation of around 175 members, the treasurer introduced transparent financial reports using plain language summaries and quarterly updates. At the same time, the church held listening sessions to explain their financial position and budgeting process. Over the next year, giving increased by 10%, and new leadership volunteers emerged. Members reported greater clarity, and surveys indicated improved trust in board decisions. Transparency didn't just improve finances — it strengthened relationships.

But clarity alone isn't enough. Conflicts of interest — real or perceived — can erode trust even when everything is technically legal. That's why the Sample Conflict of Interest Policy, also available in the ECLC, is so important. It helps ensure that: • Board members disclose relationships that could bias decisions • Treasurers and finance committee members avoid dual roles (e.g., approving their own reimbursements) • Decisions are made based on mission alignment, not influence or favoritism

In the "Good Governance" webinar (around slide 16), we see the importance of loyalty framed clearly: "Act in the best interest of the organization rather than self-interests or interests of associates." The treasurer plays a key role in upholding this — not only by avoiding conflicts, but by creating systems that prevent even the appearance of them.

When you implement this policy faithfully, you are not just protecting the church legally — you are protecting it spiritually. You are helping ensure that its decisions are pure, its witness is strong, and its members trust the process.

Another vital tool is the Trust Mapping Template, which invites boards to evaluate where trust is strong, where it's frayed, and what systems need to be clarified. It asks: • Where are people confused or frustrated with financial processes? • Where are transparency gaps? • What structures need strengthening to foster trust?

This resource, also found in the ECLC, can be used as a board retreat activity or as a reflection tool after a season of conflict or transition. It encourages open conversation about not just what's working, but what needs repair. And it helps boards move forward without blame — focusing instead on faithfulness.

Many churches experience financial disunity not because of misconduct, but because of assumptions, silence, or legacy practices that were never clarified. Treasurers who raise those questions gently, using tools like the Trust Map, become part of the church's healing — not just its management.

These tools don't require financial expertise — they require spiritual maturity. They require treasurers who understand that accountability is not just about "watching over" others — it's about serving the mission by helping the church walk in light.

This is what stewardship looks like in practice: • Truth-telling in reports • Consistency in process • Kindness in correction • Systems that reflect trust, not just compliance

And when these practices are lived out, the church becomes more than functional — it becomes credible, faithful, and free to pursue its Calling without distraction.

Conclusion and Reflection Questions

When Paul writes in 1 Corinthians 4:2, *"Now it is required that those who have been given a trust must prove faithful"* (NIV), he isn't offering a legal definition — he's offering a spiritual charge. Faithfulness isn't measured only by technical accuracy or procedural compliance. It's measured by **integrity**. By **consistency**. By whether what we say we believe is reflected in what we actually do.

That's the heart of fiduciary duty for church treasurers. It's not about fear — it's about faithfulness. You are entrusted with more than accounts. You are entrusted with the church's **financial witness**. And your leadership either builds trust — or erodes it.

But when you lead with diligence, humility, and clarity, trust grows. And as trust grows, ministry flourishes.

In *Serving the Call*, we explore how sacred responsibility is sustained through clarity and shared commitment. When the treasurer shows up prepared, transparent, and centered in purpose, they don't just "get the numbers right" — they help others see how good governance supports **faithful mission**.

And in *Embracing Our Call*, we are reminded that stewardship is not passive. It's an act of spiritual alignment. A treasurer who asks hard questions gently, who keeps reporting clear, and who consistently prioritizes what's best for the whole community is a **spiritual leader**, not just a financial one.

That's who you are becoming.

You don't need to be perfect. But you are called to be faithful.

Faithful in how you manage what has been given.

Faithful in how you uphold the board's shared duties.

Faithful in how you speak the truth — clearly, kindly, and consistently.

That is how churches stay spiritually healthy: when their leaders serve not out of fear, but from **trust, purpose, and Calling**.

Let your financial leadership reflect the heart of the Gospel — truth, grace, and a deep desire to honor what has been entrusted to you.

Because this is not just bookkeeping.
It's not just governance.

It is a sacred work.
And you are proving faithful.

🕊 Reflection Questions

1. How does 1 Corinthians 4:2 (NIV) inspire your approach to fiduciary duty?
2. In what ways does accountability reflect your spiritual calling as a treasurer?
3. How might the Trust Mapping Template, available in the ECLC, help foster clarity and trust?
4. Share a story from your experience where financial leadership, like a congregation increasing trust through transparent reporting, strengthened your church's alignment with its mission.
5. What practices can you implement to promote transparent and spiritually grounded oversight in your

Chapter 3:

Guarding the Good Deposit

Treasurers as Protectors of Calling, Not Just Currency

Guard the good deposit entrusted to you
— 2 Timothy 1:14 (NIV, adapted)

Introduction

There is more at stake in the church's finances than balanced budgets and accurate reports. Behind every dollar received and every expenditure made lies something sacred: the collective faith of a people who have trusted that their resources are being used for God's purposes. To be the one entrusted with stewarding that trust is not just a task — it is a calling.

In his second letter to Timothy, Paul charges his young protégé: "Guard the good deposit entrusted to you" (2 Timothy 1:14, NIV, adapted). This is the heart of the treasurer's work. Not merely protecting money, but safeguarding the mission. Not acting as a watchdog, but as a guardian of Calling.

Every church has received a sacred deposit — not only in offerings and accounts, but in purpose. And just as Paul warned Timothy to protect what had been entrusted to him, so too is the treasurer called to protect the integrity, transparency, and spiritual alignment of the church's financial systems.

In *Embracing Our Call*, the chapter "Building Faithful Systems" reminds us that trust is not something we hope for — it is something we build. Faithful systems are not just about control or compliance. They are about protecting the community's capacity to do what God has asked it to do. When fraud occurs, when confusion creeps in, or when silence is mistaken for stewardship, the damage is more than financial — it is relational and spiritual. This is why the treasurer's work matters so deeply.

In the "Preventing Church Fraud" webinar, the principle is clear: churches are vulnerable not because people are bad, but because systems are unclear. When roles are ambiguous, when records are inaccessible, or when trust is assumed but not built, the church becomes fragile. The treasurer's role is to strengthen that foundation.

To guard the deposit means putting systems in place that match the weight of what's being protected.

It means understanding that every bank reconciliation, every receipt policy, every expense approval is not just a formality — it's a wall of protection around the church's witness. When financial systems are weak, God's mission becomes vulnerable to mistrust. But when those systems are fortified with grace, diligence, and clarity, the church is free to move boldly into its Calling.

But protection isn't only about fraud prevention. It's also about discernment. As described in *Called Together*, protection is part of listening — attending to what's happening beneath the surface, and naming it before it grows into harm. Treasurers guard not just against dishonesty, but against drift — the quiet slide from mission toward maintenance, from purpose toward habit.

This means the treasurer may sometimes need to raise a red flag — not because something illegal is happening, but because something important is being overlooked. A ministry funded but no longer active. A pattern of staff reimbursement that's quietly shifted over time. A growing reliance on designated gifts that limits flexibility. These aren't emergencies, but they are invitations to realignment. And the treasurer, if spiritually grounded, becomes the voice that gently says, "Let's take a closer look."

This is why treasurers must see themselves not only as keepers of currency, but as protectors of Calling. You guard the integrity of the church's finances so that the integrity of its mission can flourish. You create systems that keep things clear, so that the board can lead with courage. You hold the quiet power of protection — not from fear, but from faith.

Theological Framing

To guard something sacred requires more than vigilance — it requires vision. You must know not only what you're protecting against, but what you're protecting for. In Paul's letter to Timothy, the phrase is striking: "Guard the good deposit entrusted to you"

(2 Timothy 1:14, NIV, adapted). The deposit isn't a burden. It's a treasure. A trust. A divine assignment.

This is the theology behind financial protection in the church. Treasurers are not simply managing money. They are preserving what is holy — ensuring that the resources God has provided remain aligned with the church's mission. They are holding in trust not just currency, but Calling.

In *Embracing Our Call*, the chapter "Building Faithful Systems" reminds us that systems reflect what we value. A system that is sloppy or secretive reflects disregard. A system that is clear, documented, reviewed, and prayerfully structured reflects reverence. Faithful systems are spiritual architecture — they shape and support a mission that is worth protecting.

This is why Acts 4:34 remains such a powerful standard: "There were no needy persons among them." Why? Because the early church shared all things in common, and because stewardship was not an afterthought — it was an embodiment of community and Calling. Financial systems weren't barriers to generosity. They were foundations for integrity.

This is what the treasurer protects. Not just against theft or error, but against spiritual drift. Against the subtle ways churches begin to protect themselves rather than their Calling. Against the temptation to bury or obscure the truth because it's inconvenient. When you guard the good deposit, you are guarding the church's witness to the world.

In the "Preventing Church Fraud" webinar (noted at 11:10), it's emphasized that fraud often emerges in environments of trust without verification. Churches are built on relationships — and rightly so. But trust, in biblical terms, is never blind. It is always paired with accountability. Throughout scripture, stewardship is accompanied by systems: storehouses, scribes, records, offerings counted and distributed. These are not signs of distrust — they are signs of care.

And care is the heart of this theology. To care for what God has given is an act of worship. It's why treasurers matter: they protect the future capacity of the church to act on its Calling. Not through control or suspicion, but through clarity, alignment, and truth. This spiritual posture matters most when things go quiet — when no one is asking questions, when the budget passes quickly, when the reports are accepted without review. In those moments, protection isn't reactive. It's proactive. It says, "We will not assume all is well — we will keep asking if we are aligned." That's not anxiety. That's wisdom.

In *Serving the Call*, we're reminded that trust is not an emotion — it's a system of consistent clarity. Treasurers build trust not just through competence, but through covenantal presence: showing up faithfully, reporting honestly, raising concerns with grace, and refusing to cut corners, even when no one's watching.

This is where integrity and grace meet. A treasurer with integrity holds the line. A treasurer with grace does it without shaming others. Together, these qualities reflect the heart of Christ — truth and love, both present at the table.

So when you guard the good deposit, you are not simply saying no to risk — you are saying yes to mission. You are protecting what has been entrusted so that the Spirit can move freely. You are creating the conditions where generosity can flourish, because people know their gifts will be honored. And you are modeling the kind of leadership that doesn't just build trust — it deserves it.

Practical Application

If the treasurer's role is to guard the church's deposit, then their most essential tools are the systems that keep that deposit secure. This is where ministry meets process — not as a departure from faithfulness, but as its expression. To protect the church's financial integrity is to protect its ability to act on its Calling. That is holy work.

The most common financial risks churches face aren't dramatic scandals — they are slow erosions of clarity. Reimbursement processes that evolve informally. Bank accounts with too few signers. Expense decisions made by text message. These small cracks often go unnoticed until trust breaks down or damage is done. The treasurer's ministry is to notice them before that happens — and to lovingly insist on better practices.

The Financial Policies & Procedures Template, available in the Effective Church Leadership Community (ECLC), offers clear guidance. It affirms that good policy is not about suspicion — it is about building faithful systems that make integrity easier and missteps harder. Core practices include:

· Requiring dual signatures on checks above a certain threshold
· Segregating duties for deposits, bookkeeping, and reconciliation
· Keeping receipts on file for all staff reimbursements
· Conducting regular internal audits

None of these practices are about bureaucracy. They are about protection. And not just of the money — but of the people.

Church fraud is a pervasive threat, with studies estimating more money is stolen annually from congregations than spent on global missions. Audits reveal that 95% of nonprofit fraud goes unreported, often due to weak controls like solo cash counting or missing oversight. These lapses not only drain resources but erode trust, hindering ministry. The Sample Whistleblower Protection Policy and dual-counting procedures from the ECLC can prevent such losses, protecting both funds and the church's witness, as *The Ministry of Money* emphasizes.

A small rural church of about 80 members learned this lesson firsthand. For years, the Sunday offering was counted alone by one trusted volunteer, with no second witness or written record. After a congregant raised quiet concerns, the board adopted the Sample Whistleblower Protection Policy and implemented dual-counting using rotating teams. Within months, giving increased, and congregational surveys showed an 85% rise in trust. With restored confidence, the church launched a new community meal ministry — a visible sign of trust transformed into mission.

In the *Preventing Church Fraud* webinar (at 18:50), we learn that most fraud happens not in malice, but in isolation. When someone is struggling, under pressure, or unaccountable, even a well-meaning person can drift. Strong systems protect both the church and its servants from that risk. The treasurer leads by setting those systems in place — and by making sure they're followed with kindness and consistency.

That's where the Sample Document Retention Policy, also found in the ECLC, becomes crucial. Many churches hold on to records far too long or dispose of them too soon. But keeping clear timelines — for donation receipts, financial statements, grant documentation, and personnel files — reduces confusion and ensures readiness during reviews, transitions, or audits. These simple practices communicate: We are trustworthy. We are organized. We are ready.

Equally vital is the Sample Whistleblower Protection Policy, which ensures that anyone in the church — staff, board, or congregation — can safely report concerns. A treasurer who champions this policy isn't sowing fear. They are creating safe space for truth. They are helping ensure the church's systems are strong enough to withstand scrutiny and compassionate enough to invite honesty.

Stories shared in the *Preventing Church Fraud* transcript confirm this. Churches who had "trusted the wrong person" often realized, too late, that it wasn't trust that failed — it was a lack of process. No second signer. No review of credit card charges. No written procedures. Treasurers must learn from these patterns and build strength before the storm.

That strength isn't just logistical. It's spiritual. In *Called Together*, we're reminded that discernment happens in systems, not just in moments. When the financial structure is sound, the board is free to lead with courage. When the paperwork is in place, generosity flows without hesitation. When expectations are clear, staff serve with freedom, not fear.

And when fraud or failure does occur, systems allow for recovery — not collapse. Treasurers who have built healthy procedures make restoration possible. They give the church a way back.

This is what it means to guard the good deposit: to build systems that are worthy of the mission they protect. That means setting the policies, reviewing them annually, teaching others how to follow them, and — when necessary — holding the line with compassion. When a treasurer quietly implements controls that protect a staff member from temptation, when they document procedures so the next leader won't feel lost, when they speak up to stop a harmful practice before it takes root — they are doing holy work.

And it is work the whole church will never see, but always feel. Because when finances are handled with integrity, the church walks lighter, gives freer, and trusts deeper.

Conclusion and Reflection Questions

Some will say the treasurer's job is to track the money. And yes — you track every line, every statement, every deposit and withdrawal. But the sacred part of your work is not in the counting. It's in the guarding. You are guarding not just funds, but faithfulness. You are safeguarding the systems that preserve mission integrity and enable spiritual courage.

2 Timothy 1:14 says it plainly: "Guard the good deposit entrusted to you" (NIV, adapted). This verse wasn't written to a treasurer, but to a spiritual leader. Still, it fits — because you, too, are a spiritual leader. And what you've been entrusted with is more than spreadsheets. You've been entrusted with the church's credibility, capacity, and Calling.

In *Serving the Call*, sacred responsibility is the constant refrain. Not as pressure, but as purpose. Treasurers are not expected to carry it all. But they are expected to show up with integrity, to ask good questions, to name risks with grace, and to refuse to let silence masquerade as stewardship.

In *Embracing Our Call*, the invitation is to build systems that reflect trust. Not just because they work — but because they're worth believing in. A church with strong systems is a church that honors its people. It doesn't rely on goodwill alone. It builds safety, clarity, and freedom into its processes — so that the Spirit can move without confusion or fear.

This is what you protect.

You protect the community's ability to serve, to give, and to risk without losing sight of what matters most. You protect the relationships that make generosity possible. You protect the truth from becoming obscured, and the future from being compromised by today's shortcuts.

And you do it with grace. With consistency. With hope.

You may never be applauded from the pulpit. But your presence matters more than you know. Because when the financial systems are guarded with care, the church can move boldly into its mission. When the paperwork is clean and the records are clear, the board can make wise decisions. And when the treasurer leads with quiet, humble courage, the whole body becomes more free.

So guard the deposit. Not in fear, but in faith. Not with suspicion, but with clarity. Not for yourself — but for the mission God has entrusted to your community.

That's the heart of the work. That's the soul of stewardship.

🕊 Reflection Questions

1. How does 2 Timothy 1:14 (NIV, adapted) inspire your role in protecting the church's mission?
2. In what ways does safeguarding the church's deposit reflect your spiritual calling?
3. How might the Financial Policies & Procedures Template, available in the ECLC, strengthen your church's integrity?
4. Share a story from your experience where protective measures, like a church restoring trust through fraud-preventing controls, preserved the church's mission.
5. What steps can you take to ensure your oversight safeguards both currency and calling?

Part II

Systems That Safeguard

The integrity of the upright guides them...
– Proverbs 11:3

Chapter 4:

Faithful in Little, Faithful in Much

The Spiritual Practice of Financial Detail

Whoever can be trusted with very little can also be trusted with much, and whoever is dishonest with very little will also be dishonest with much
– Luke 16:10 (NIV)

Introduction

No one joins a church to manage spreadsheets. And yet, some of the holiest work in the life of a congregation happens quietly in ledgers, reconciliations, and budget margins. It's the work that keeps the lights on, yes — but more importantly, it's the work that keeps the community honest, humble, and clear about what it values. This is the treasurer's realm.

Jesus's words in Luke 16:10 are not merely a lesson in ethics — they are a profound statement of spiritual principle: "Whoever can be trusted with very little can also be trusted with much" (NIV). It's a reminder that faithfulness begins in the details. And for the church treasurer, details are the front line of ministry.

The theme of Part One — A Calling Entrusted — is not only about holding big responsibilities. It's about holding small ones faithfully. The check that gets signed. The decimal that gets double-checked. The report that gets reviewed one more time before it's shared. These tasks may not be glamorous, but they are sacred — because they are acts of care. They say, "This matters. Our mission matters. The people who gave these funds matter."

In *Embracing Our Call*, the chapter "Financial Clarity as Spiritual Practice" frames this beautifully: attention to detail is not just a professional skill — it is an act of reverence. It shows that we believe God is present even in the fine print. When treasurers approach their tasks with this mindset, the work becomes more than administrative. It becomes a form of worship.

But it isn't always easy.

Some treasurers find themselves overwhelmed by the tediousness of the role — managing records, reconciling inconsistencies, explaining reports to a board that doesn't always understand or appreciate the work. Others face the challenge of maintaining accuracy under pressure — with limited time, shifting expectations, or inherited spreadsheets that feel like puzzles missing key pieces. Still, in all of this, detail remains the way forward. As the *Building*

Financial Literacy Among Church Leaders webinar affirms (at 12:15), clarity begins with tracking what's true — not just in total balances, but in the lines and ledgers that reveal how the church is moving through its Calling. Good stewardship doesn't start with surplus. It starts with accuracy.

This chapter explores what it means to treat financial detail not as drudgery, but as a spiritual discipline. It avoids the frameworks we've already explored in earlier chapters — this isn't about interpreting mission, managing fiduciary duty, or preventing fraud. This is about the small, faithful habits that shape how the church operates every day.

And it's about how treasurers, through their meticulous attention, help others walk in confidence.

When the budget is accurate, leaders can plan without fear.

When the reports are clear, decisions are made with integrity.

When the books are in order, the Spirit has room to move.

That is not just administration — it is ministry.

Theological Framing

If you want to know whether someone understands stewardship, watch how they handle small things. Not the grand gestures, but the daily acts — the way they label receipts, follow procedures, or prepare a monthly report. These aren't just technical details. They are the quiet proof of whether someone has internalized the sacredness of what they've been given.

Jesus's words in Luke 16:10 cut to the core: "Whoever can be trusted with very little can also be trusted with much" (NIV). The inverse is also true — disregard in the small things undermines trust in the big ones. In church leadership, this principle is not just practical — it's deeply spiritual. The treasurer who approaches details with reverence isn't just doing their job — they are shaping the church's witness.

In *Embracing Our Call*, "Financial Clarity as Spiritual Practice" elevates detail as a discipline. Not because perfection is required, but because attentiveness is holy. The goal is not flawless execution. The goal is faithfulness. When treasurers honor small responsibilities — reconciling accounts, tracking petty cash, checking for duplicate entries — they model what it means to take God's provision seriously.

This attention to detail is more than bookkeeping. It's a theology of care. It says: nothing given to the church is too small to be honored. No act of generosity is too minor to be tracked well. No financial obligation is too simple to be fulfilled with care. When a treasurer lives by that standard, they teach the entire church what trustworthiness looks like — not by preaching, but by quietly keeping things honest.

The Parable of the Talents in Matthew 25:14–30 makes this clear. The master doesn't ask his servants to multiply fortunes overnight. He asks them to be faithful with what they were given. The one who hid the money wasn't rebuked for stealing — but for avoiding responsibility. He treated the master's trust as a burden rather than a charge. The lesson for treasurers is this: faithfulness is not passive. It engages. It accounts. It works with what's been given and prepares it for what's to come.

This is why financial clarity is an act of worship. It's not just about understanding — it's about stewarding well. In *Serving the Call*, clarity is consistently emphasized as a foundation for trust and leadership. Churches thrive not because they avoid risk, but because they operate with confidence — and confidence is born from clarity.

This clarity isn't only for those with a finance background. It's for anyone willing to treat detail as devotion. Treasurers who lead with this mindset bring peace to every meeting. They reduce anxiety by increasing accuracy. They make complex decisions possible by delivering honest data. They make giving joyful because members can see exactly how funds are used.

All of that begins in the smallest tasks.
The way reports are labeled.
The consistency of formatting.
The care taken in double-checking figures.
The calm with which discrepancies are investigated — not ignored.
Each act is a brushstroke in a larger picture — a picture that says, "We are trustworthy. We are accountable. We are walking with God's provision in our hands, and we are treating it like it matters." That's theology in action. And it belongs to every treasurer who opens QuickBooks or Excel or a handwritten ledger and chooses to see those numbers as sacred.

Practical Application

Attention to financial detail isn't glamorous. It's rarely celebrated. And yet, in the life of a church, it is one of the most consequential forms of service. When a treasurer consistently tends to the fine points — the line items, the formulas, the budget notes — they are making ministry possible. Not flashy ministry. Faithful ministry. One of the most useful tools in this work is the Budget Template, available in the Effective Church Leadership Community (ECLC). It's a guide that helps treasurers and finance teams move through the budget with intentional care — not just at year-end, but throughout the year. By asking questions like:
• Are we spending according to priorities?
• Are we tracking designated gifts accurately?
• Are overages and underspending being discussed?

This checklist doesn't just catch errors — it illuminates patterns. It prompts reflection, not just accounting. It keeps small oversights from becoming larger problems, and helps teams stay aligned on both values and financial realities.

A mid-sized urban church with around 200 members was struggling with missing documentation — incomplete receipts, unclear notes, and inconsistent reporting. The finance committee adopted the Sample Financial Dashboard Template and the Clarity Worksheet Template from the ECLC. Within a few months, records became consistent, meetings more productive, and congregational trust rose significantly. This clarity allowed them to revise their budget more confidently and launch a new initiative for young adult ministry that had long been delayed due to financial uncertainty.

The *Building Financial Literacy Among Church Leaders* webinar (at 21:40) affirms this exact point: clarity begins with consistency. A treasurer who routinely prepares clean, digestible reports is doing more than satisfying a requirement. They are making discernment possible. Reports that are too complex, inconsistent, or overly technical often cause confusion — or worse, avoidance. When data is hard to trust, decisions suffer. But when data is clear, ministry can move forward with confidence.

That's where the Sample Financial Dashboard Template, also found in the ECLC, becomes invaluable. It provides a visual summary of key data points — revenue, expenses, cash flow, giving trends — in a format board members can grasp quickly. Dashboards don't replace detailed reports, but they open the conversation. They help board members see where attention is needed and give them a frame for asking better questions.

This kind of clarity builds energy. People engage more freely when they feel informed and empowered. And that starts with how the data is presented — not just accurate, but understandable.

To deepen that connection, the Clarity Worksheet Template can be used as a bridge between financial data and mission alignment. Also available in the ECLC, this tool allows leadership teams to ask whether their spending patterns reflect what God is calling them to do. Unlike the checklist or dashboard, this tool isn't just technical — it's spiritual. It invites discernment.

That's what the practice of detail does — it doesn't just correct; it guides.

Detail also becomes critical during transitions. When a treasurer steps down or a finance chair rotates off, having clear, consistent systems in place allows the next leader to step in with confidence. Documentation isn't just paperwork — it's part of the church's memory. The best treasurers know this and keep records not just for themselves, but for those who will come after them.

And all of this — checklists, dashboards, worksheets, documentation — can be seen as holy tools. Not because the tools themselves are sacred, but because they protect and communicate what is.

Financial detail is how we tell the truth. And in churches, where stories matter, that truth builds credibility, compassion, and community.

Conclusion and Reflection Questions

There is nothing small about faithfulness.

Jesus said, "Whoever can be trusted with very little can also be trusted with much" (Luke 16:10, NIV). That's not a proverb — it's a paradigm. It means the smallest acts of stewardship carry the full weight of Calling. Every cell in the budget. Every figure in the ledger. Every entry in the general journal. They all matter — because they all reveal how deeply we honor what has been entrusted to us.

For treasurers, that means showing up not just with accuracy, but with attentiveness. Because behind every number is a gift. A decision. A hope. An offering made in faith. The role of treasurer, then, is not just about handling money. It is about honoring the trust behind every dollar.

In *Embracing Our Call*, we are reminded that financial clarity is a spiritual practice. Not because clarity itself is holy, but because it leads us toward integrity, collaboration, and discernment. When reports are clear, people are less anxious. When processes are transparent, boards are more courageous. When data is accurate, decisions are more faithful.

And when treasurers lead with clarity, they make all of that possible.

Serving the Call teaches that sacred responsibility is not about perfection. It's about posture. Treasurers don't have to be experts in every tool. But they must be committed — to understanding the numbers, to sharing them in ways others can follow, and to double-checking even the smallest details because those details shape the entire financial story.

When you practice faithfulness in the small things, you make space for the Spirit to move in the big things.

A well-formatted report can calm a tense meeting.

A single dashboard can ignite fresh vision.

A reconciled account can build trust that has long been fractured.

A question asked about a line item can uncover a deeper need.

This is how you serve. Quietly. Faithfully. Clearly.

So take heart in your spreadsheets. Take joy in your formatting. Take pride in reconciling the numbers, not because it's glamorous, but because it's good. And goodness, in the church, is never wasted.

You are building trust, one detail at a time.

You are cultivating clarity that will outlast your tenure.

You are making faithfulness visible — not in theory, but in practice.

And you are helping the church remember: If we can be trusted with little, we will be ready for more.

❦ Reflection Questions

1. How does Luke 16:10 (NIV) inspire your approach to financial detail as a treasurer?
2. In what ways does meticulous financial oversight reflect your spiritual calling?
3. How might the Sample Financial Dashboard Template, available in the ECLC, enhance clarity in your church's finances?
4. Share a story from your experience where attention to detail, like a church improving trust through clear financial records, strengthened the church's mission.
5. What steps can you take to ensure your financial practices build trust through clarity?

Chapter 5:

To Whom Much Is Given

The Weight and Wonder of Financial Responsibility

From everyone to whom much has been given, much will be required; and from the one to whom much has been entrusted, even more will be demanded
— Luke 12:48 (NRSV)

Introduction

The role of a church treasurer carries a weight that goes beyond numbers. It is a sacred trust, a responsibility to steward the resources God has entrusted to the congregation. Luke 12:48 reminds us: "From everyone to whom much has been given, much will be required..." (NRSV). For treasurers, this means not only managing funds but ensuring they serve the church's mission with integrity and wisdom.

This chapter explores the spiritual and practical dimensions of financial responsibility. It's about recognizing the magnitude of what's been entrusted and rising to meet it with diligence, clarity, and faith.

Theological Framing

The call to stewardship is a call to accountability. Luke 12:48 sets a high standard: those given much must give much in return. For treasurers, this is not a burden but a privilege — a chance to align every financial decision with God's purpose. In *Embracing Our Call*, we see stewardship as a spiritual practice, requiring attentiveness to both the practical and the holy.

Scripture does not separate the sacred from the administrative. In fact, it elevates responsibility as a defining trait of faithful leadership. Treasurers are called not simply to preserve assets, but to advance the church's mission with wisdom. Their diligence enables others to trust that resources are being handled in alignment with God's call.

Practical Application

Financial stewardship demands more than balancing the books — it requires systems that reflect the church's values. The Financial

Policies & Procedures Template from the Effective Church Leadership Community (ECLC) provides a framework for responsible management, ensuring transparency and accountability. It clarifies processes for disbursements, reimbursements, authorizations, and reporting, giving treasurers and boards the shared language and structure they need to lead with confidence.

A small suburban church of about 90 members realized they had no formal review process for their monthly financial statements. The treasurer submitted reports, but the board rarely discussed them, leading to passive oversight and occasional financial surprises. With help from the ECLC's Financial Policies & Procedures Template, the church adopted new structures requiring board-level review each month. As a result, board engagement increased, financial decisions improved, and trust between staff and leadership grew. Today, their meetings include regular reflection on whether financial patterns are supporting the church's Calling — a culture shift that began with one small change.

Oversight is not about suspicion — it's about shared responsibility. When boards regularly review reports, ask clarifying questions, and engage in budget discussions, they affirm that stewardship is a communal act. The treasurer may prepare the documents, but financial faithfulness belongs to the whole leadership body.
That's why healthy policies matter. They aren't just about what to do when things go wrong — they're about how to ensure things go right. When roles are clear, timelines are set, and procedures are followed, the board and treasurer can move from reactive to proactive.
Treasurers can also use these policies as onboarding tools. New finance committee members and board leaders are often eager to help but unsure where to begin. A shared policy document provides guidance, expectations, and a sense of shared mission. It ensures that energy is channeled into wise, mission-aligned decisions — not confusion or correction.

And when something does go wrong — an error in a report, an unapproved expenditure, a missed deadline — the policy provides a path forward. It removes blame and replaces it with process. It allows for grace without sacrificing clarity.

This is part of the sacred weight treasurers carry: not to control, but to guide. Not to take on the work alone, but to ensure that systems allow others to carry it with them. That is what it means to be faithful in much.

Conclusion and Reflection Questions

The weight of financial responsibility is not meant to overwhelm — it is meant to form. When Jesus said, "Much will be required," he was not describing punishment. He was describing Calling. To be given much is to be trusted. To be trusted is to be accountable. And to be accountable is to become more faithful over time.

As a treasurer, your task is not simply to perform. It is to form. To form systems that protect mission. To form teams that lead with clarity. To form habits that build trust. And to form a church culture that treats every dollar as a sacred tool for ministry.

The more we are given, the more we can give — not just in resources, but in responsibility. Financial leadership is not about perfection, but about purpose. It is a ministry of trust, and like all ministries, it thrives when practiced with care, consistency, and courage.

You don't carry this Calling alone. With tools, support, and the Spirit's guidance, you can lead with faith and finish each month with peace.

You are not just handling money. You are answering God's call. And much will come from it.

🕊 Reflection Questions

1. How does Luke 12:48 (NRSV) shape your understanding of financial stewardship?
2. In what ways does responsible financial management reflect your spiritual calling?
3. How might ECLC tools, like the Financial Policies & Procedures Template, enhance your church's stewardship?
4. Share a story from your experience where financial oversight, like a church improving decisions through board reviews, strengthened stewardship.
5. What steps can you take to ensure your financial oversight aligns with the church's calling?

Chapter 6:

Honor the Lord with Your Wealth

Cultivating a Culture of Generosity

Honor the LORD with your wealth and with the first of all your crops. Then your barns will be filled with plenty, and your vats will burst with wine.
– Proverbs 3:9–10 (CEB)

Introduction

There's a subtle shift that happens when a church moves from managing its finances to celebrating its generosity. When money stops being only about expenses and starts becoming a spiritual expression. When giving is no longer a transaction, but a response to grace.

This shift doesn't happen by accident. It's cultivated — slowly, intentionally, prayerfully — often through the steady influence of one particular voice: the treasurer. Not because they give the most, or even speak the most, but because their posture sets the tone. How they talk about money, report on giving, and invite the congregation into financial clarity has a profound impact on the church's collective spirit.

Proverbs 3:9–10 offers this invitation: "Honor the LORD with your wealth and with the first of all your crops. Then your barns will be filled with plenty, and your vats will burst with wine" (CEB). This is not a prosperity promise — it's a principle. When generosity flows from trust and reverence, there is enough. Not always abundance in the worldly sense, but enough for the mission. Enough for the moment. Enough to remind us that God provides.

This chapter explores how treasurers help build that culture. Not just by balancing reports or managing pledges, but by fostering joy in giving. It is a shift from scarcity to Spirit. From anxiety to alignment.

In *Embracing Our Call*, the chapter "Generosity as Spiritual Practice" emphasizes that giving is a form of worship. It's not just something we do to fund ministry — it is ministry. The way a church invites, receives, and celebrates giving reflects its theology. And the treasurer, often without fanfare, becomes the one who ensures that theology stays grounded in truth, transparency, and grace.

But that's not always easy. Many churches carry old wounds around money — seasons of fear, financial missteps, or giving campaigns that felt more like pressure than invitation. Treasurers often walk into these histories and must gently help the church begin again — rebuilding trust through clarity, calm, and consistent practices.

The challenges are real:
- How do we speak about giving without sounding transactional?
- How do we encourage generosity without evoking guilt?
- How do we share financial information without overwhelming people?

These aren't logistical questions — they're pastoral. And the treasurer plays a quiet pastoral role, shaping how the church answers them.

With the right tools and a clear heart, the treasurer can lead the church into a new culture — one marked by gratitude, generosity, and grace.

Theological Framing

Giving is not an afterthought in scripture. It is not a footnote to discipleship. It is a central practice of worship — a way to acknowledge who God is and what God has provided. Proverbs 3:9–10 says, "Honor the LORD with your wealth and with the first of all your crops. Then your barns will be filled with plenty, and your vats will burst with wine" (CEB). The invitation here is not about transaction, but about relationship. We give because we trust. We give because we've been blessed. We give because giving places God at the center.

When treasurers help congregations honor God with their wealth, they are doing more than tracking income — they are facilitating a sacred rhythm. They are helping the church express its love, its hope, and its mission in tangible form. Generosity becomes a way the body worships together.

In *Embracing Our Call*, "Generosity as Spiritual Practice" reminds us that giving is an act of spiritual maturity. It is not just a budgetary necessity — it is a reflection of how deeply a church believes that

God will continue to provide. And that belief becomes visible in the way the church invites its members to give, how it uses what is given, and how it celebrates the act of giving.

The apostle Paul expands this theology in 2 Corinthians 9:6–8 (CEB): "The one who sows sparingly will also reap sparingly, and the one who sows generously will also reap generously. Everyone should give whatever they have decided in their heart. They shouldn't give with hesitation or because of pressure. God loves a cheerful giver. God has the power to provide you with more than enough for every kind of good work." (See Appendix A for scripture references.)

What's striking in Paul's words is not the promise of provision — though it's there — but the tone of freedom and joy. Giving isn't to be coerced. It's to be released from the heart. And treasurers, more than most, create the structures that either support or hinder that release.

When churches struggle financially, it's easy for giving to become a point of pressure. "We need more." "We're behind." "Let's push this month." But these approaches, however well-meaning, often disconnect giving from grace. They turn generosity into obligation. Theologically, that's not just ineffective — it's misaligned.

Treasurers help the church return to its theological roots by ensuring that the invitation to give is consistent with the church's trust in God. That doesn't mean ignoring real needs. It means framing those needs with faith, not fear.

- Instead of "We need you to give more," say: "Here's what your giving makes possible."
- Instead of "We're short again," say: "Here's where we've seen your generosity bear fruit."
- Instead of "We're trying to meet a goal," say: "We're inviting you into the mission."

This isn't spin — it's spiritual framing. And the treasurer has a voice in how that story is told.

This is the sacred task of cultivating generosity. It's not manipulation. It's not maintenance. It is, in the deepest sense, discipleship. And when treasurers approach their work as an extension of that discipleship, they help the whole church live into its calling — not just with its words, but with its wealth.

Practical Application

A culture of generosity doesn't begin with a campaign. It begins with a mindset — and that mindset is shaped over time through clarity, transparency, and trust. The treasurer plays a central role in this shaping. Not through flashy presentations or emotional appeals, but through consistent, faithful leadership that builds confidence in the giving process.

One of the most powerful tools to support this work is the Sample Stewardship Campaign Guide, available in the Effective Church Leadership Community (ECLC). This resource helps churches develop seasonal or annual campaigns that reflect their mission and invite participation without pressure. It provides prompts and frameworks that turn the stewardship conversation into a spiritual journey:

- Why does giving matter in this season?
- What impact has generosity already made?
- How can each household be part of this work, no matter their income level?

Instead of focusing on deficits, these campaigns center on purpose. They speak from abundance, not anxiety. They make giving feel like joining something holy, not paying dues.

But campaigns are only one piece. Treasurers build trust when they lead with transparency. That's where the Sample Financial Transparency Report, also in the ECLC, becomes invaluable. Unlike technical financials that require interpretation, this tool distills key data into digestible, mission-oriented language:

- What was received?
- What was spent — and why?
- What ministry outcomes were supported?

When reports are shared in clear, accessible ways — with visuals, narratives, and honest commentary — giving increases. Not because people are manipulated, but because they see the story their dollars are telling.

A mid-sized rural church of about 150 members discovered they had incomplete records of past donations, leaving both givers and leaders uncertain about the accuracy of their reports. Using the Sample Financial Transparency Report from the ECLC, they began issuing quarterly summaries that highlighted giving patterns, ministry results, and key updates. As trust grew, giving increased — not from pressure, but from participation. Members began sharing stories of how they felt more connected and confident knowing exactly how their generosity was making a difference.

This type of transparency also reduces suspicion. It calms anxiety. And it opens the door to new givers, who may feel hesitant about contributing to an institution they don't fully understand. Clarity breeds confidence. And confidence nurtures generosity.

Equally important is the tone in which giving is acknowledged. The Sample Donor Acknowledgment Letter, available in the ECLC, provides a model rooted in gratitude rather than transaction. It reminds givers that:

- Their contribution is valued
- Their trust is honored
- Their giving is making a difference

Letters like these may seem simple, but they have long-term effects. Givers who feel appreciated are more likely to remain engaged. They give not just again, but more joyfully — because they know they are seen.

These tools — campaigns, reports, acknowledgments — are all part of a wider pattern: building a relationship between the giver and the mission. Treasurers nurture that relationship when they advocate for transparent communication, when they ask how reports are shared publicly, when they encourage leadership to tell giving stories with warmth and integrity.

A culture of generosity doesn't emerge from pressure. It grows from shared purpose, clarity, and gratitude. And treasurers are the quiet architects of that growth.

Conclusion and Reflection Questions

At its heart, generosity is not about how much we have — it's about how we honor what we've been given. Proverbs 3:9–10 doesn't just instruct us to give. It calls us to give first — and to give with reverence: "Honor the LORD with your wealth and with the first of all your crops. Then your barns will be filled with plenty, and your vats will burst with wine" (CEB). That's not just a stewardship principle — it's a posture of the soul.

As treasurer, your influence in this space is quiet, steady, and powerful. You don't have to lead the campaign or speak from the pulpit to shape a culture of generosity. You shape it every time you prepare a report that tells the truth with grace. Every time you advocate for clarity. Every time you ensure a donor is thanked. Every time you frame giving as a reflection of faith, not a response to fear.

In *Embracing Our Call*, we are reminded that generosity is a spiritual practice — something formed over time in community. The treasurer plays a key role in forming that practice, not through exhortation, but through systems that invite trust, language that reflects joy, and processes that make giving feel connected to God's work in the world.

You do this best when you:

Speak from abundance, not scarcity

Celebrate every gift as a reflection of trust

Build consistent habits of reporting and transparency

Encourage the church to see its resources as a tool for mission

This is how barns are filled. Not because we demanded more, but because we created space for the Spirit to move — and invited others to join.

There is no one right way to lead generosity in your church. But there is a faithful way: with courage, clarity, and kindness. With the willingness to speak honestly about what's needed — and with the faith to believe that God has already placed enough in our hands. Your leadership makes that faith visible. And your presence — quiet though it may be — becomes a signal to the church:
We will honor what we've been given. We will share it wisely. And we will do so with joy.

🕊 Reflection Questions

1. How does Proverbs 3:9–10 (CEB) inspire your role in fostering a culture of generosity?
2. In what ways does promoting generous giving reflect your spiritual calling as a treasurer?
3. How might the Sample Stewardship Campaign Guide, available in the ECLC, encourage generosity in your church?
4. Share a story from your experience where transparent financial practices, like a church boosting giving through clear reporting, inspired generosity.
5. What steps can you take to cultivate a culture of generosity through your financial leadership?

Part III

Telling the Truth in Numbers

You yourselves are our letter… written not with ink but with the Spirit…
— 2 Corinthians 3:2

Chapter 7:

You Cannot Serve Two Masters

Aligning Financial Decisions with God's Calling

"No one can serve two masters... You cannot serve both God and wealth."
– Matthew 6:24 (CEB)

Introduction

Financial stewardship in the church requires a singular focus: serving God's mission. Matthew 6:24 warns, "No one can serve two masters... You cannot serve God and wealth" (NRSV). For treasurers, this means ensuring financial decisions prioritize the church's calling over competing interests. This chapter explores how treasurers can lead with clarity and faith to keep mission at the center of every financial choice.

In congregational life, this clarity can be difficult to maintain. Competing voices, urgent needs, and informal traditions can shift a church's attention away from the mission. Sometimes, even well-meaning decisions are made to avoid conflict or accommodate convenience — not to fulfill Calling. That's why treasurers are not just financial managers; they are mission interpreters. Their leadership reminds the board and congregation: the budget is a tool for discernment, not a compromise between preferences.

Faithful stewardship means making decisions that serve God alone — not institutional survival, not individual influence, and certainly not ease. That's why the role of the treasurer is as spiritual as it is practical.

Theological Framing

Serving God alone is a call to align resources with divine purpose. Matthew 6:24 challenges treasurers to avoid the lure of wealth's security, focusing instead on God's kingdom.

Financial leadership requires honesty about where our loyalties lie. When financial decisions begin to prioritize familiarity, tradition, or comfort, the church slowly shifts its trust from Spirit to strategy. The treasurer's job is to help the congregation course-correct — not with confrontation, but with clarity.

In *Embracing Our Call*, stewardship is described as a spiritual discipline. This means our decisions about money are not just managerial — they are formational. When we allocate funds based on God's leading rather than preference, we reinforce that our trust is in God. When we delay a purchase to spend time discerning its purpose, we show reverence for what has been given.

The call to serve God alone does not ask the treasurer to avoid systems — it invites them to use systems that serve Calling. That distinction is essential. Systems are not the enemy of mission. Systems allow the mission to be protected from distraction, drift, and disorganization.

When treasurers ground their leadership in this spiritual commitment, they help the whole church practice its faith — not only in worship, but in every financial decision.

Practical Application

Serving God alone requires systems that prioritize mission over convenience or personal gain. The Financial Policies & Procedures Template from the Effective Church Leadership Community (ECLC) helps treasurers establish clear processes for budgeting, approvals, and reporting, ensuring decisions align with the church's calling.

A mid-sized rural church with about 175 members had long operated on trust alone. Expense approvals were informal, reimbursements were verbal, and financial decisions were often made without review or reflection. Over time, inconsistencies emerged and tensions rose. With support from the ECLC's Financial Policies & Procedures Template, the church implemented formalized approval processes, clarified responsibilities, and trained staff and volunteers on new procedures. In just six months, financial confusion decreased, trust was restored, and the board reported greater freedom to focus on mission rather than micromanaging money.

Treasurers do not serve two masters when their practices are consistent, documented, and shared. Informal traditions may feel easier in the moment, but they often mask deeper issues — assumptions, expectations, and occasionally, unresolved power dynamics. Clear policy is not just a financial safeguard — it's a spiritual commitment to unity.

When financial practices are vague, personalities fill the gap. But when they are clear, purpose fills the room. Boards spend less time debating process and more time discerning priorities. Staff and volunteers feel safe knowing what is expected. Donors feel confident that their gifts are being used with integrity.

This kind of alignment frees the church to act boldly. When the systems support the mission, new ideas are less risky. The church can invest in ministry with confidence, knowing there's a structure in place that will keep it grounded in wisdom.

The treasurer's role in this is not to be the gatekeeper, but the guide. Policies and procedures are not ends in themselves — they are tools for enabling faithful action. When used wisely, they clear a path for generosity, focus, and spiritual freedom.

This is how we serve God alone: not by rejecting financial systems, but by ensuring those systems are in service to something greater.

Conclusion and Reflection Questions

Serving God alone transforms financial stewardship into worship. Matthew 6:24 calls treasurers to lead with unwavering focus, ensuring resources serve the church's mission.

This is not about austerity. It's about alignment. It's about the quiet discipline of returning to the question: Are we making this decision because it is right, or because it is easy?

The treasurer helps the church stay accountable to that question. Not with judgment, but with hope. With a steady reminder that trust in God does not mean carelessness — it means courage.

When a church commits to financial practices that are clear, mission-centered, and Spirit-led, it reflects the heart of Matthew 6:24. It refuses to serve the systems themselves — and insists that systems serve the call.

That's what treasurers do: they clear away the clutter, so that the church can hear its calling clearly. And then — they help it walk in that direction with confidence.

🌱 Reflection Questions

1. How does Matthew 6:24 (NRSV) shape your approach to financial stewardship?
2. In what ways does prioritizing mission reflect your spiritual calling?
3. How might ECLC tools, like the Financial Policies & Procedures Template, strengthen your church's focus?
4. Share a story from your experience where structured financial practices, like a church streamlining processes with clear policies, prioritized mission.
5. What steps can you take to ensure your financial practices serve God alone?

Chapter 8

Building Trust Through Transparency

Fostering Integrity in Financial Stewardship

"Behold, you delight in truth in the inward being, and you teach me wisdom in the secret heart."
– Psalm 51:6 (ESV)

Introduction

Financial transparency is not just a practice — it's a reflection of the church's integrity. Psalm 51:6 declares, "Behold, you delight in truth in the inward being…" (NRSV). For treasurers, this means leading with honesty and clarity in all financial matters, ensuring the church's actions align with its values. This chapter explores how treasurers foster trust through transparent reporting and accountability, making integrity visible in every financial decision. Transparency requires more than the availability of information — it requires intentional communication. A congregation cannot respond faithfully to what it does not understand. Treasurers are called to remove barriers, not just to share numbers, but to share meaning. When the inner workings of financial life are accessible to the whole body, trust grows. Integrity becomes visible, and the church can move forward together with clarity and peace.

Theological Framing

Truth in financial stewardship is a spiritual commitment. Psalm 51:6 calls the church to inward honesty, reflected outwardly in clear, truthful practices. In *Embracing Our Call*, transparency is a form of worship, showing the congregation that God's provision is managed with reverence. Treasurers uphold this truth, building trust that strengthens the church's witness.

When leaders communicate openly about finances, they do more than meet a fiduciary obligation — they model what it means to walk in the light. Financial transparency can defuse conflict, strengthen discernment, and unite a congregation in purpose. But secrecy, even if unintentional, undermines trust. When financial information is hidden, irregular, or unclear, it invites speculation. Transparency, by contrast, invites partnership. It signals that leadership is trustworthy and that the congregation is respected.

When a church aligns its inner life with its outward witness — when financial truth is spoken clearly, regularly, and without fear

— it reflects the heart of Psalm 51. It delights the God who calls the community to honesty, humility, and shared purpose.

Practical Application

Transparency in financial stewardship requires systems that make truth accessible. The Sample Financial Transparency Report from the Effective Church Leadership Community (ECLC) helps treasurers present clear, mission-focused financial updates, fostering trust and accountability.

A small urban church of about 80 members struggled with inconsistent financial reporting. Updates came sporadically, and congregants were unsure how giving was being used or what the church's financial status truly was. The treasurer implemented the Sample Financial Transparency Report from the ECLC, committing to regular, easy-to-read quarterly updates that highlighted giving, spending, and ministry outcomes. Over time, members expressed increased trust and began engaging more actively in stewardship conversations. Leadership reported that decisions improved because the congregation was better informed and more united.

Regular, meaningful reporting doesn't require advanced software or large teams. What it does require is intentionality. The Sample Financial Transparency Report offers a framework for this kind of intentionality:
- It simplifies key numbers into understandable language.
- It connects financial trends to ministry outcomes.
- It invites reflection, not just reaction.
- It fosters curiosity instead of confusion.

Treasurers can use this tool to shift the financial conversation from anxiety to alignment. Instead of waiting until there's a shortfall, transparency becomes proactive. Reports show not just where the church stands — but where it's headed, and how its resources are helping it get there.

Transparency also nurtures resilience. When the inevitable challenges arise — a sudden repair, a decline in giving, or a delayed grant — the congregation is already in the habit of engaging financial truth. Surprises are fewer, and when they come, they are met with shared responsibility.

This level of transparency does more than inform — it forms. It forms a congregation that sees financial clarity as part of spiritual maturity. It forms leadership habits that reflect courage and trust. And it forms a culture where telling the truth is normal — even when that truth includes uncertainty.

That is what it means to delight in truth in the inward being.

Conclusion and Reflection Questions

Truth in the inward being transforms financial stewardship into a testament of faith. Psalm 51:6 calls treasurers to lead with transparency, ensuring the church's integrity shines through every decision.

A treasurer doesn't need to have all the answers — but they must be willing to tell the truth. That is the heart of integrity: not perfection, but honesty. And honesty, in the financial life of the church, is what builds a bridge between faith and trust.

When leaders speak the truth about giving, expenses, needs, and opportunities, the church grows in its capacity to respond with wisdom. And when systems are in place to communicate that truth clearly, the church's mission gains strength and focus.

Financial transparency is not about full access to every line item — it's about telling the story faithfully, consistently, and clearly. It's about helping the congregation see how their generosity is being used for God's purposes.

That's the kind of integrity God delights in. And that's the kind of leadership the church needs.

🌱 Reflection Questions

1. How does Psalm 51:6 (NRSV) inspire your approach to financial transparency?
2. In what ways does transparent stewardship reflect your spiritual calling?
3. How might ECLC tools, like the Sample Financial Transparency Report, enhance your church's trust?
4. Share a story from your experience where transparent reporting, like a church enhancing trust with clear financial updates, strengthened integrity.
5. What steps can you take to ensure your financial practices reflect inward truth?

Chapter 9

Envisioning Abundance: Financial Wisdom for God's Mission

Cultivating a Legacy of Faithful Stewardship

"His master said to him, 'Well done, good and faithful servant. You have been faithful over a little; I will set you over much. Enter into the joy of your master.'"
— Matthew 25:21 (ESV)

Introduction

The treasurer's role is a calling to serve faithfully, ensuring the church's resources advance its mission. Matthew 25:21 celebrates the "good and faithful servant" who stewards well (NRSV). This chapter explores how treasurers embody this service through diligent financial management, serving not for recognition but to honor God's trust. It's about leading with humility and commitment, making every financial decision a reflection of faithful service.

Faithfulness, in this context, is not about perfection. It's about consistency. It's about showing up — month after month, year after year — with a heart that seeks not control, but care. Faithful treasurers don't just manage money; they create conditions for ministry to flourish.

Theological Framing

Faithful stewardship is an act of service to God and community. Matthew 25:21 calls treasurers to manage resources with integrity and diligence, reflecting God's trust. In *Embracing Our Call*, stewardship is a ministry, where faithfulness in financial tasks strengthens the church's mission. Treasurers serve not for praise but to enable God's work through the congregation.

This parable from Matthew affirms that what matters is not how much we've been given, but how we've handled it. Whether managing $100 or $1 million, the same call applies: Be faithful. Be clear. Be consistent.

Service in this context is not glamorous. It happens in spreadsheets and statements. In late nights reconciling accounts and early mornings preparing for finance committee meetings. But it is service nonetheless — holy work, done on behalf of others, with the humility that says, "This is not mine. I am a caretaker of what belongs to God."

Practical Application

Faithful stewardship requires systems that ensure diligent management. The Financial Policies & Procedures Template from the Effective Church Leadership Community (ECLC) supports treasurers in creating clear, accountable processes for budgeting, approvals, and reporting, fostering trust and efficiency.

A large rural church of about 350 members had strong giving and a committed treasurer, but weak internal controls. One person handled deposits, disbursements, and recordkeeping with no regular review. Concerns about oversight began to surface. Using the ECLC's Financial Policies & Procedures Template, the church implemented segregation of duties, required dual approvals for large expenses, and scheduled quarterly reviews by the finance committee. Within the year, trust increased, processes improved, and the board reported greater clarity and peace of mind.

Faithfulness in financial management means resisting shortcuts. It means doing things the right way even when no one is watching. Systems like the ones found in the ECLC template are not about bureaucracy — they're about protecting the integrity of the ministry.

This includes:
- Clear roles for financial oversight
- Written procedures for disbursements and approvals
- Consistent reporting rhythms for transparency
- Documentation that honors the trust of the congregation

None of these are flashy. But all of them are powerful. They create a rhythm of reliability — and over time, that rhythm becomes the heartbeat of a trustworthy church.

Treasure is not measured only in offerings. It is measured in the community's ability to trust leadership, to risk generosity, and to engage God's mission without fear of mismanagement. Treasurers help build that trust, one procedure at a time.

Faithfulness also shows up in preparation. The treasurer who arrives early to meetings, who reviews reports in advance, who double-checks their work — that person is not just efficient. They are practicing stewardship as spiritual discipline. They are showing the congregation what it means to take responsibility seriously. And that kind of quiet leadership shapes the entire culture of a church. It invites others to lead with similar care — whether in music, mission, or maintenance. The church becomes a place where faithfulness is normal, not exceptional.

Conclusion and Reflection Questions

Faithful service transforms financial stewardship into ministry. Matthew 25:21 calls treasurers to lead with diligence, ensuring resources serve God's mission. By serving humbly, you inspire the church to trust and act boldly in faith.

This is not about doing it all. It's about doing your part with integrity. It's about bringing your best, even when no one sees. It's about remembering that the spreadsheets you prepare, the policies you uphold, and the decisions you guide are all part of a larger story — a story of faithfulness that God is writing through the church.

The church needs faithful servants. Not just preachers and teachers, but treasurers who carry the quiet weight of integrity. Who show up when it's hard. Who organize what's needed. Who make it possible for others to give, to serve, and to lead.

That's the ministry of money. And when you serve with that heart, the words of Jesus echo still: "Well done, good and faithful servant."

🕊 Reflection Questions

1. How does Matthew 25:21 (NRSV) inspire your approach to financial stewardship?
2. In what ways does faithful service reflect your spiritual calling?
3. How might ECLC tools, like the Financial Policies & Procedures Template, enhance your church's stewardship?
4. Share a story from your experience where structured financial controls, like a church strengthening trust with clear processes, enhanced faithful stewardship.
5. What steps can you take to ensure your financial practices reflect faithful service?

Chapter 10

Sustaining Mission: Financial Resilience for God's Work

Adapting with Faith in Changing Seasons

"And my God will supply every need of yours according to his riches in glory in Christ Jesus."
– Philippians 4:19 (ESV)

Introduction

Financial stewardship is about more than meeting today's needs — it's about sustaining the church's mission for the future. Galatians 6:9 encourages, "Let us not grow weary in doing what is right..." (NRSV). This chapter explores how treasurers ensure long-term mission impact through strategic financial management, balancing present demands with future vision.

The work of financial leadership can feel unending. Month after month, reports must be prepared, budgets reviewed, and decisions made. But beneath that rhythm lies something holy: a commitment to preserving the church's Calling. Sustaining mission means seeing beyond the present — recognizing that what we build now, with diligence and wisdom, becomes the foundation for the next generation's ministry.

Theological Framing

Sustaining mission requires perseverance and faith. Galatians 6:9 calls treasurers to steward resources with endurance, ensuring the church's mission thrives. In *Embracing Our Call*, stewardship is a commitment to God's ongoing work, aligning finances with eternal purposes. Treasurers sustain mission by fostering stability and trust. This kind of faithfulness is not reactive — it is proactive. It looks ahead, prepares for uncertainty, and makes decisions not just based on what is urgent, but on what is important. It asks: Will this choice strengthen our ability to serve in five years? Will it help us respond to God's call with freedom, not fear?

Theologically, sustaining mission is an act of trust. We are not just maintaining institutions — we are tending to what God has planted. Financial stability becomes the trellis on which the mission can grow, adapt, and bear fruit over time.

Practical Application

Sustaining mission demands systems that support long-term financial health. The Financial Policies & Procedures Template from the Effective Church Leadership Community (ECLC) helps treasurers establish robust processes for budgeting, oversight, and reporting, ensuring mission continuity.

A mid-sized suburban church of about 200 members had no regular structure for reviewing budgets once they were approved. Financial oversight was inconsistent, and leaders felt disconnected from how resources supported ministry. Using the ECLC's Financial Policies & Procedures Template, the church implemented quarterly board reviews, clarified reporting responsibilities, and adopted a year-end evaluation process. As a result, budgeting became more collaborative, priorities became clearer, and the church reported renewed focus on aligning spending with its mission.

Strategic budgeting is not just about numbers — it's about alignment. Clear review processes ensure that spending reflects Calling, not convenience. The ECLC template provides a structure that empowers boards to stay engaged, ask good questions, and support the treasurer's work with shared responsibility. Key practices include:

- Establishing regular financial review schedules
- Clarifying roles and responsibilities for oversight
- Documenting budget assumptions and priorities
- Evaluating financial decisions through a mission lens

When these practices are in place, the church can move from maintenance to momentum. Instead of reacting to shortfalls or unexpected costs, leaders can anticipate needs, plan wisely, and invest confidently in the work God is calling them to do.

This kind of stability is deeply spiritual. It allows the congregation to give generously, knowing their gifts are managed with care. It allows staff and volunteers to plan boldly, knowing the church will stand behind them. And it allows the community to grow in faith — not driven by anxiety, but rooted in trust.

Sustaining mission is not about saving money — it's about stewarding it well so that the mission is never held back by confusion, hesitation, or lack of clarity. The treasurer is the quiet leader who helps make that possible.

Conclusion and Reflection Questions

Sustaining mission transforms stewardship into a legacy of faith. Galatians 6:9 calls treasurers to lead with perseverance, ensuring resources serve God's purpose. By fostering financial stability, you empower the church to pursue its mission boldly.

This work is not always celebrated. It may not get applause or public recognition. But it is work that matters. It holds the church steady in uncertain times. It prepares the ground for what's next. And it honors the God who entrusted us with this Calling.

When treasurers lead with patience, clarity, and vision, they embody the kind of leadership Galatians 6:9 points toward: steadfast, faithful, and unshaken by weariness.

So take courage. Stay the course. Keep showing up — report by report, meeting by meeting, season by season. You are sustaining more than finances. You are sustaining mission.

ꙮ Reflection Questions

1. How does Philippians 4:19 (ESV) inspire your role in fostering financial resilience for your church's mission?
2. In what ways does adaptive stewardship reflect your spiritual calling as a treasurer?
3. How might a financial resilience plan strengthen your church's mission sustainability?
4. Share a story from your experience where adaptive financial decisions sustained the church's calling.
5. What steps can you take to build financial resilience in your church?

Part IV

Budgets That Bear Witness

Write the vision; make it plain…
Habakkuk 2:2

Chapter 11

Cheerful Givers

Budgets That Reflect Our Calling

"God loves a cheerful giver."
— 2 Corinthians 9:7 (ESV)

Introduction

The church's budget is more than a spreadsheet—it's a story. It reveals what we value, what we prioritize, and what we believe God is calling us to do in the world. And while the numbers may change year to year, the deeper purpose remains: to craft a financial plan that reflects the church's mission and inspires joyful giving.

Paul's encouragement in 2 Corinthians 9:7 offers a glimpse into the heart of Christian stewardship: *"God loves a cheerful giver"* (see Appendix A). Giving that is offered freely, with joy and conviction, is a spiritual act. And yet, it is difficult for people to give cheerfully when the church's financial life feels disconnected from its sense of call.

Psalm 90:12 grounds us in that connection: *"So teach us to number our days that we may get a heart of wisdom"* (see Appendix A). Budgeting requires wisdom—not just about how money flows, but about how time, energy, and spiritual commitment are directed. The treasurer plays a crucial role in guiding the church toward this kind of wisdom.

One church had long budgeted by looking back: repeating last year's numbers with minor adjustments. But when they began to ask what God was calling them to prioritize, everything changed. Outreach became a central focus. Their budget shifted to reflect this, investing in community meals, justice partnerships, and a part-time outreach coordinator. Congregants responded—not just with increased giving, but with renewed energy. They saw themselves in the story the budget was telling.

This chapter explores how budgeting can become a tool of transformation—not only in how funds are spent, but in how the church discerns its direction. It invites treasurers to see budgeting as a spiritual discipline, and to help the church move from survival-based planning to mission-driven hope.

Theological Framing

The call to cheerful giving in 2 Corinthians 9:7 is more than a directive—it's a glimpse into the kind of community God longs for: one where generosity flows not from pressure or guilt, but from joy, freedom, and purpose. The phrase *"Each one must give as he has decided in his heart, not reluctantly or under compulsion"* speaks to discernment. It calls the community to give in response to the Spirit, not to anxiety.

This is where the church's budget becomes sacred. It's not only a financial document—it's a testimony of what the church has heard from God. When the numbers reflect that calling, giving becomes joyful, because it feels meaningful.

Psalm 90:12 adds another layer: *"Teach us to number our days that we may get a heart of wisdom."* The church budget, in this sense, is a reflection of stewardship not only over money, but over time. It asks, how will we use the season we've been given? What does faithfulness look like now? Budgeting with wisdom means choosing what matters most, and trusting that when the church invests in its calling, provision will follow.

One church struggling with declining youth participation paused to ask how their budget might support the next generation. The answer didn't come in a line item, but in prayerful reflection. Over the course of three months, they restructured existing funds to support a part-time youth coordinator, funded a weekend retreat, and set aside a modest scholarship fund for camps. The result was not just better programs—it was a renewed sense of purpose.

Another church that once feared deficits found new courage when they reframed their budget process. Instead of starting with limits, they started with listening. They asked what ministries had borne fruit, what longings were emerging, and what God might be asking them to risk. The budget became a map of that discernment. Not every line was funded as fully as hoped, but every line told a story. And that story gave people a reason to give with joy.

This is the treasurer's sacred role—to help the church listen, reflect, and respond. Not just to numbers, but to God's voice. Budgets shaped in this way are not burdens—they are invitations. They help the community live with wisdom and give with gladness.

Practical Application

Budgets that reflect the church's calling don't emerge by accident. They are shaped through practices that invite discernment, center the mission, and engage the whole community in spiritual conversation. The treasurer's role in this process is not only technical—it is deeply pastoral.

One congregation restructured its budget after realizing that its current format obscured its priorities. Though outreach was named as a core value, it received less than 5% of annual spending. After reviewing this disconnect, the board collaborated with ministry teams to draft a new structure organized by mission areas: worship, outreach, discipleship, and care. The revised budget didn't immediately increase funding, but it clarified the conversation—and it paved the way for new investment in community ministry the following year.

Another church chose to engage the congregation in its budgeting process. Rather than presenting a finished draft at the annual meeting, they held two listening sessions. Members shared stories of where they saw God moving and named what mattered most to them. The treasurer worked with the finance committee to integrate that input. When the final budget was presented, people recognized their voice in it. That recognition translated into new pledges and renewed trust.

A third congregation experienced a shift in mission focus after welcoming a refugee family. What began as a short-term effort became a long-term ministry. The church's leadership realized that the budget needed to reflect this change. They revised mid-year allocations, redirecting discretionary funds and building a new line for immigration ministry. Though small, the change signaled commitment—and the community responded with joy.

Finally, a church seeking to inspire generosity transitioned to a narrative budget. Instead of spreadsheets, they created a visual document that showed how giving supported lives transformed through worship, outreach, and formation. Testimonials were included alongside each section. The result was not only increased giving, but greater participation. People felt connected to the story the church was telling.

Each of these examples shows how budgeting can become an act of shared vision. The treasurer is not simply presenting numbers. You are helping the church discern its identity—and fund it with integrity. Even the use of a budgeting tool available in church leadership communities can be helpful to begin the shift toward mission-centered budgeting, but it is the posture that makes the difference.

This work invites the church to trust that the joy of giving emerges not from pressure, but from purpose. When people see how their contributions connect to the mission, they give with their hearts, not just their wallets.

Conclusion and Reflection Questions

Mission-driven budgeting is not about balance alone. It is about faithfulness. It is about listening well and responding with clarity. As treasurer, you are entrusted with more than reports—you are entrusted with helping the church articulate what it believes and how it intends to live that belief into the world.

Paul's words in 2 Corinthians 9:7 remind us that cheerful giving is not naive. It is a fruit of spiritual clarity. It grows when people see how their giving aligns with God's work through the church. Psalm 90:12 offers similar wisdom: we do not budget to control the future, but to steward the season we've been given.

If your church is ready to take the next step:

- **Develop a mission-driven budget plan.** Begin with a conversation about calling. Invite leaders to reflect on where the church is being led and align your budget process accordingly.
- **Host a congregational budget visioning session.** Create space for members to share their hopes, name what matters most, and see how their giving supports the whole.

Budgets that reflect God's calling don't just balance the books. They tell the truth about who we are—and who we long to be.

🌱 Reflection Questions

1. How does 2 Corinthians 9:7 (ESV) inspire your role in crafting budgets that reflect your church's calling?
2. In what ways does mission-driven budgeting reflect your spiritual calling as a treasurer?
3. How might aligning your budget with your church's mission inspire cheerful giving?
4. Share a story from your experience where a mission-driven budget strengthened the church's calling.
5. What steps can you take to ensure your budget reflects your church's God-given purpose?

Chapter 12

Not In Vain

Transparent Budget
Planning Processes

"Unless the Lord builds the house, those who build it labor in vain."
— Psalm 127:1 (ESV)

Introduction

Planning without purpose may still produce a budget—but it may not produce fruit. When churches make financial plans behind closed doors, disconnect budget decisions from discernment, or rush through timelines without engaging hearts, trust erodes and mission drifts. In contrast, transparent budgeting is not just a technical practice—it is a spiritual one. It invites the whole church to build with God.

Psalm 127:1 sets the tone for this chapter: *"Unless the Lord builds the house, those who build it labor in vain"* (see Appendix A). The task of the treasurer is not merely to plan—it is to help the community build in alignment with God's call. And that cannot happen if decisions are hidden, rushed, or overly controlled. Proverbs 15:22 reinforces this: *"Without counsel plans fail, but with many advisers they succeed"* (see Appendix A).

One church began holding annual budget workshops open to the entire congregation. The purpose was not to vote, but to learn together. Members heard from ministry leaders, asked honest questions, and offered input. Over time, these sessions built trust and reduced resistance during formal votes. Giving increased, not because of pressure, but because people believed in the process.

This chapter explores the spiritual and practical importance of transparent budget planning. It names the quiet ways mistrust creeps in and offers tools to open the process—fostering not only better outcomes, but deeper faith.

Theological Framing

True financial stewardship begins with spiritual intention. Psalm 127:1 reminds us that even well-structured plans will falter if they are not rooted in God's guidance: *"Unless the Lord builds the house, those who build it labor in vain"* (see Appendix A). This doesn't mean we abandon structure—it means we center the planning process in prayer, wisdom, and shared discernment.

That discernment is not meant to be private. Proverbs 15:22 urges us: *"Without counsel plans fail, but with many advisers they succeed"* (see Appendix A). Wisdom grows in community. This is not just a governance value—it is a theological one. Budget planning becomes a spiritual act when it draws on the insight, hopes, and faithful reflections of the people God has called together.

Transparency in budgeting reflects our trust in one another and our collective trust in God. When churches make space for participation—not just approval—budgeting shifts from transaction to transformation. The board is still responsible for final decisions, but they are no longer making those decisions alone.

One church applied this principle when deciding whether to invest in a new children's ministry program. Rather than make the decision solely in the finance and board meetings, the leadership hosted a discernment conversation open to all families. Insights from that conversation led them to revise their proposal and include a rotating volunteer stipend in the budget—a small line that made a big difference in implementation. The final plan passed unanimously, not because everyone agreed on every detail, but because the process was shared.

Transparent budgeting is not about broadcasting every discussion—it is about ensuring that the process invites wisdom and builds trust. It is about making room for God to speak through many voices, and ensuring that what we build reflects the heart of the whole community.

Practical Application

Transparency in budget planning isn't just about sharing numbers—it's about fostering trust, clarifying mission, and honoring the call to shared stewardship. When church leaders invite the community into the budgeting process, they model openness and embody the kind of discernment that builds unity.

One large urban congregation began holding annual budget workshops open to all members. The goal was not to vote line-by-line, but to listen and learn together. The treasurer, newly installed and passionate about transparency, facilitated sessions where ministry leaders shared their hopes and financial needs for the coming year. Attendees asked honest questions—about giving trends, outreach spending, and building maintenance. Through these conversations, priorities emerged. Youth programming was increased by 15%, supported by broader enthusiasm and clarity about its impact. Giving rose 10% the following year, not because of pressure, but because of partnership.

Over time, these budget workshops changed the culture of the congregation. Members came to see budgeting not as a bureaucratic necessity, but as a shared spiritual practice. The treasurer was no longer seen as a gatekeeper but as a guide—helping the church discern how to use its resources faithfully.

Other congregations may not host full workshops, but simple steps can still increase transparency: previewing draft budgets with ministry teams, sharing clear summaries with the congregation, and using narrative explanations to show how money supports mission. Each of these actions tells a story: not just about dollars, but about faith in action.

Transparent budgeting is about more than compliance. It reflects what we value, how we trust one another, and who we believe ourselves to be.

Conclusion and Reflection Questions

The difference between a budget and a ministry plan is not the format—it is the spirit behind it. When treasurers foster transparent planning processes, they become co-builders with God. They help create a space where discernment can flourish, where mistrust can be healed, and where financial stewardship reflects the Spirit's leading.

Psalm 127:1 reminds us that without God's presence at the center, even our most efficient structures fall short. And Proverbs 15:22 affirms that wise planning includes many voices. A budget may be approved by a board—but its strength comes from how it is discerned.

If your church is ready to build not in vain, begin with two invitations:

- **Implement a transparent budget planning process.** Review your timeline, decision points, and communication practices. Look for places to invite openness and participation.
- **Host a budget transparency forum.** Invite members to learn how the budget is shaped, what values guide it, and how they can be involved. Let it be more than informational—let it be formational.

When the process reflects our shared trust in God and one another, the result is not only a better budget—it's a stronger church.

🌱 Reflection Questions

1. How does Psalm 127:1 (ESV) inspire your role in building transparent budget planning processes?
2. In what ways does open budget planning reflect your spiritual calling as a treasurer?
3. How might collaborative budgeting practices strengthen trust and shared mission in your church?
4. Share a story from your experience where transparency transformed your church's approach to finances.
5. What steps can you take to foster clarity, inclusion, and discernment in your budgeting process?

Chapter 13

Estimate The Cost

Cash Flow and Discernment in Budget Planning

"Suppose one of you wants to build a tower. Won't you first sit down and estimate the cost to see if you have enough money to complete it?"
— Luke 14:28 (NIV)

Introduction

In the ministry of money, building with intention is an act of faithfulness. Financial planning is not just about tracking expenses or approving budgets. It's about seeing ahead, discerning what will be needed in future seasons of ministry, and ensuring that the resources to fulfill God's call will be present when the time comes.

Jesus' words in Luke 14:28 offer a grounding principle: *"Suppose one of you wants to build a tower. Won't you first sit down and estimate the cost to see if you have enough money to complete it?"* (see Appendix A). The heart of this teaching is not about building projects—it's about spiritual wisdom. Churches that commit to ministry without understanding the timing and pacing of their financial capacity often find themselves overcommitted and underprepared.

Proverbs 21:5 adds a powerful complement: *"The plans of the diligent lead surely to abundance, but everyone who is hasty comes only to poverty"* (see Appendix A). Financial foresight is not a lack of faith—it is an act of stewardship. And for treasurers, this means more than preparing a static budget. It means paying attention to cash flow: the rhythms, risks, and reserves that help the church move sustainably through the year.

One church committed to a bold outreach initiative—launching a weekday community meal and hospitality program. The ministry aligned deeply with their mission, but within months, expenses began to outpace income. The treasurer realized that while the total budget was sound, the timing of income was not. By implementing a cash flow projection and restructuring how reserve funds were accessed, the church was able to stay faithful to its mission while avoiding a financial crisis.

This chapter explores the role of cash flow discernment in faithful budget planning. It invites treasurers to look beyond the annual plan and to consider how spiritual vision and financial pacing must go hand in hand.

Theological Framing

Luke 14:28 invites a pause. Jesus asks his listeners to consider the cost—not as a deterrent to discipleship, but as a grounding for it. He knew that passion alone cannot sustain a vision. There must also be preparation. In the financial life of the church, this means we do not presume resources will always be there simply because our cause is righteous. We take the faithful step of looking ahead.

To "sit down and estimate the cost" is an act of trust. It places the spiritual value of wisdom above the temptation to rush forward. The wisdom literature echoes this in Proverbs 21:5: *"The plans of the diligent lead surely to abundance, but everyone who is hasty comes only to poverty."* Haste may appear as faith—but it is often anxiety in disguise.

This perspective invites a deeper discernment about timing. What if waiting is not delay, but wisdom? What if postponing a program or project is not failure, but faithful pacing?

One congregation had been preparing to launch a capital campaign for sanctuary renovations. Excitement was high, and the need was real. But as they began reviewing cash flow projections, the treasurer and leadership team recognized a mismatch between projected giving patterns and anticipated construction costs. Rather than rush forward, they paused the launch. In the next six months, they hosted community conversations, cultivated new pledges, and adjusted the scope of work to align with sustainable phases. When the campaign resumed, the congregation was not only ready—they were unified.

In these moments, the treasurer serves as a spiritual steward—not by saying "no" to faith, but by saying "yes" to wise preparation.

Another church discerned a call to invest in young adult ministry. The idea was affirmed enthusiastically. But after a review of cash flow timing, the treasurer proposed a delay until late summer, when pledge income historically increased. In the meantime, a modest fund was seeded to prepare. By the time the initiative launched, there was not only excitement—but stability.

Cash flow discernment reminds us that planning is not a one-time event—it is a rhythm. God builds in seasons, and the church is healthiest when its finances reflect that.

Practical Application

Cash flow discernment is not a spreadsheet exercise—it is a ministry of foresight. It helps the church steward what has been entrusted with clarity and care, so that ministry can flourish without the anxiety of financial surprises. One of the treasurer's sacred tasks is helping the board see not only what is true today, but what is likely to come.

A mid-sized suburban church committed to launching a weekday community meal and hospitality program—offering hot lunches, prayer space, and connection for anyone in need. The call was clear, and the congregation responded generously to initial appeals. But within months, expenses began to outpace income. Volunteers were serving faithfully, but the weekly cost of food, utilities, and staffing strained the church's regular operations. The program was at risk of closure.

The treasurer, sensing the urgency but refusing to panic, offered a different path. With support from a small working group, they developed a 12-month cash flow projection—mapping monthly inflows, regular giving patterns, and recurring expenses. The projection revealed a seasonal shortfall: giving typically declined during the summer months, and without adjustments, the program would become unsustainable by July.

Rather than abandon the ministry, the board used this data for discernment. They approved a temporary reserve transfer, delayed non-essential spending, and launched a mid-year giving campaign tied directly to the impact of the hospitality ministry. By September, giving had increased, and the program was operating with a stable foundation—serving over 50 families weekly.

This experience reshaped how the church viewed financial leadership. The treasurer had not "saved the program" alone—they had empowered the board to see the full picture. Cash flow discernment became a regular part of their decision-making process. Now, every new ministry initiative includes a cash flow plan before launch, ensuring the excitement of vision is matched by the wisdom of planning.

Key practices for faithful cash flow management include:

- Developing 6–12 month cash flow projections that account for seasonal trends
- Monitoring and adjusting projections at least quarterly to reflect updated realities
- Building and protecting cash reserves as a buffer during income fluctuations
- Encouraging boards to pair bold mission with realistic pacing and fiscal visibility

Treasurers are not prophets, but they are interpreters of patterns. By revealing those patterns early, they give the board time to act not out of fear, but in faithful response. Cash flow is more than timing—it is truth-telling about capacity. And truth, shared in love, makes space for lasting ministry.

Conclusion and Reflection Questions

Estimating the cost is not about shrinking our vision—it is about honoring it. The treasurer's role is to ensure that dreams are built on steady ground, that discernment includes timing, and that the mission has both spiritual clarity and financial foresight.

Luke 14:28 calls us to count the cost—not to avoid the work, but to complete it well. And Proverbs 21:5 assures us that diligence leads to abundance. These truths belong in the sanctuary, the board room, and the spreadsheet.

If your church is ready to build with greater confidence:

- **Develop a cash flow projection plan.** Include 12-month forecasts, timing assumptions, and potential gaps. Review and update regularly with your finance team.
- **Host a cash flow discernment workshop.** Invite leaders to reflect on seasonal rhythms, reserve practices, and how faith informs financial pacing.

When planning and provision walk hand in hand, the church is ready to meet the moment with grace.

🕊 Reflection Questions

1. How does Luke 14:28 (NRSV) inspire your role in stewarding your church's resources with foresight and care?
2. In what ways does using cash flow projections reflect your spiritual calling as a treasurer?
3. How might proactive financial planning support your church's ability to respond to God's call with boldness?
4. Share a time when cash flow discernment helped your church sustain a ministry that was at risk.
5. What steps can you take to integrate seasonal and long-term cash flow analysis into your board's financial practices?

Part V

Serving Faithfully to the End

Let us not grow weary in doing good…
— Galatians 6:9

Chapter 14

What You Owe

Compliance as Stewardship

"Pay to all what is due them—taxes to whom taxes are due, revenue to whom revenue is due, respect to whom respect is due, honor to whom honor is due."
– Romans 13:7 (NRSVUE)

Introduction

Stewardship includes fulfilling legal and ethical obligations. Matthew 22:21 calls the church to "render therefore to Caesar the things that are Caesar's..." (NRSV). This chapter explores how treasurers ensure compliance with regulations, from taxes to employment laws, aligning financial practices with integrity and mission.
For many churches, compliance can feel like a distraction from ministry — a tangle of paperwork and policies. But when we view it through the lens of stewardship, it becomes clear that compliance is not about control. It's about witness. It's about showing the world that the church can be trusted — with money, with people, and with truth.

Theological Framing

Compliance is a form of faithful stewardship. Matthew 22:21 reminds treasurers to honor legal obligations while serving God. In *Embracing Our Call*, compliance is a spiritual discipline, reflecting the church's commitment to truth and justice. Treasurers uphold this by ensuring financial practices meet regulatory standards.
This is not a secondary task. It is part of our public witness. Just as we care for the sanctuary or prepare worship with excellence, we are called to tend to our legal responsibilities with diligence. When the church models integrity in how it pays staff, manages records, or files tax documents, it proclaims a gospel of trustworthiness.
Faithful compliance does not mean perfection. It means responsiveness. It means humility in the face of complexity. It means acknowledging when something needs to be corrected — and taking action to make it right.

Practical Application

Compliance requires diligent systems to meet legal requirements. The ECLC's compliance checklist supports treasurers in navigating tax, payroll, and employment regulations, ensuring integrity. For example, a small church misclassified a worker as a contractor, risking penalties. The treasurer corrected filings, aligning with regulations.

A mid-sized urban church of about 200 members discovered they had misclassified a part-time janitor as an independent contractor instead of an employee. After reviewing the ECLC's compliance checklist, the treasurer led a process to correct the error, reclassify the position, and file amended forms. The staff person was transitioned onto payroll with proper withholdings, and the church received praise from the board for taking responsibility. Members expressed increased trust in the church's financial practices, and the experience became a turning point in how the church viewed stewardship and accountability.

These situations are more common than we think. In many churches, especially those with legacy systems or long-standing staff, policies are based more on habit than on law. But habit is not enough to ensure compliance.
Treasurers must be willing to ask hard questions:

- Are we classifying people correctly?
- Are we issuing 1099s or W-2s appropriately?
- Are we tracking time, withholdings, and reimbursements inline with the law?
- Are we prepared for an audit or review?

The ECLC compliance checklist walks treasurers through each of these areas. It's not just a tool for protection — it's a guide to faithfulness. When churches follow best practices, they not only reduce legal risk — they model excellence, justice, and care for those who serve.
This includes things like:

- Written employment agreements for all paid staff
- Up-to-date job descriptions and wage classifications

- Documented approval processes for reimbursements
- Regular review of payroll filings and deadlines

Compliance isn't exciting. But it is essential. When treasurers attend to these systems with humility and care, the church becomes more trustworthy — and its witness grows stronger.

Conclusion and Reflection Questions

Compliance transforms stewardship into a witness of integrity. Matthew 22:21 calls treasurers to lead with diligence, ensuring the church honors its obligations. By fostering compliance, you strengthen trust and mission.

Churches should never fear truth. When we embrace our responsibilities and align our practices with both Spirit and statute, we become stronger. We remove distractions. We build trust. And we create the conditions for our mission to flourish — not just today, but for years to come.

Faithful stewardship is not limited to budgeting and generosity. It extends to every policy, every form, every time we sign a paycheck or file a report. And in doing these things well, we echo the voice of Jesus: Render to Caesar what is Caesar's — and to God, what is God's.

🌱 Reflection Questions

1. How does Matthew 22:21 (NRSV) inspire your approach to compliance?
2. In what ways does compliant stewardship reflect your spiritual calling?
3. How might ECLC tools, like the compliance checklist, enhance your church's integrity?
4. Share a story from your experience where compliance, like a church correcting misclassification, strengthened stewardship.
5. What steps can you take to ensure your financial practices meet legal standards?

Chapter 15

Silence The Ignorant

Governance and Compliance

"For the Lord's sake accept the authority of every human institution, whether of the emperor as supreme, or of governors, as sent by him to punish those who do wrong and to praise those who do right."
– 1 Peter 2:13–14 (NRSV)

Introduction

Governance is a cornerstone of faithful stewardship, ensuring the church's mission is protected. 1 Peter 2:15 calls the church to "put to silence the ignorance of the foolish" through good deeds (NRSV). This chapter explores how treasurers uphold governance, aligning financial practices with mission through clear policies and oversight.

When governance is strong, the church is steady. Its decisions are accountable. Its leaders are trusted. But when governance falters — when roles are unclear or reviews are inconsistent — the community's confidence weakens. That's why treasurers are essential to the governance process. Not only do they manage the numbers, but they help ensure the systems surrounding those numbers are clear, just, and trustworthy.

Theological Framing

Governance reflects the church's commitment to integrity. 1 Peter 2:15 calls treasurers to lead with diligence, ensuring governance practices silence doubts through transparency. In *Embracing Our Call*, governance is a spiritual act, safeguarding the church's mission. Treasurers strengthen trust by fostering accountable systems.

The scripture reminds us that the church's defense is not in clever words or strict control, but in doing good. Good governance is one of the ways the church "does good." When policies are followed, decisions are documented, and responsibilities are shared, the church sends a message: this community can be trusted. We are not perfect — but we are responsible.

That kind of trust is not automatic. It is earned over time through systems that prioritize clarity, justice, and alignment with mission. And treasurers are often the ones who guide those systems quietly, faithfully, and with deep spiritual purpose.

Practical Application

Effective governance requires systems that ensure accountability. The ECLC's governance checklist supports treasurers in establishing clear policies for oversight, approvals, and reporting. For example, a church faced a bylaws conflict over financial authority, resolved through a governance review.

A large suburban church with about 400 members discovered that credit card statements were not being regularly reviewed. While purchases were legitimate, the lack of oversight led to growing concerns from the finance committee. Using the ECLC's governance checklist, the church established monthly financial reviews, added receipt documentation requirements, and created a reporting flow between staff and board. Within six months, giving increased and congregational trust was visibly strengthened — not because the problem was large, but because the response was faithful.

Oversight does not imply suspicion — it expresses stewardship. When boards regularly engage in reviews, set clear expectations, and follow their own policies, they reinforce that integrity matters. The ECLC governance checklist provides a roadmap for this:
• Defining roles between staff and board
• Clarifying thresholds for approvals
• Establishing review timelines for financial reports and credit cards
• Ensuring that bylaws match current practices and are followed

Good governance doesn't happen by default. It happens when treasurers, pastors, and board members collaborate with humility, clarity, and consistency.

That is what silences the ignorant — not force, but faithfulness.

Conclusion and Reflection Questions

Governance transforms stewardship into a witness of trust. 1 Peter 2:15 calls treasurers to lead with integrity, ensuring the church's mission endures. By fostering governance, you silence doubts and empower ministry.
In a world where institutions are increasingly questioned, good governance is one of the church's strongest witnesses. It tells the truth about who we are: a people who care about justice, accountability, and the responsible use of God's gifts.
Treasurers who engage in governance do more than serve — they protect. They ensure that every dollar, every policy, and every decision is wrapped in prayer, clarity, and alignment with Calling. This is not about power — it's about faithfulness. And faithfulness, done well and done quietly, has the power to silence even the strongest critics..

🕊 Reflection Questions

1. How does 1 Peter 2:13–14 (NRSV) inspire your role in fostering governance and compliance as a treasurer?
2. In what ways does robust governance reflect your spiritual calling as a steward?
3. How might strong governance practices strengthen your church's public witness?
4. Share a story from your experience where governance efforts advanced the church's mission.
5. What steps can you take to ensure your church's governance aligns with its mission and legal standards?

Chapter 16

What Is Right

Revenue-Generating Activities vs. Purpose

"For we aim at what is honorable not only in the Lord's sight but also in human sight."
– 2 Corinthians 8:21 (NRSVUE)

Introduction

In seasons of financial strain, churches often turn to creativity. A bake sale here, a building rental there, a craft fair, a silent auction. These revenue-generating activities help fill budget gaps—but they also invite deeper questions: What is the purpose behind these efforts? Do they reflect who we are? And do they align with what we are called to do?

2 Corinthians 8:21 offers a compass: "For we aim at what is honorable not only in the Lord's sight but also in human sight." As treasurers, we hold the responsibility of ensuring that financial practices reflect both legal integrity and spiritual character. That's especially true when the church earns income outside of tithes and offerings.

One church learned this while managing a growing stream of rental income from their fellowship hall. Initially, it was a few community groups and birthday parties. But as demand grew, so did the revenue—and so did the complexity. Questions arose about unrelated business income tax, facility use priorities, and the impact on the church's identity. The treasurer stepped in not only to assess legal risks but to guide the board in reflecting on the spiritual implications. They re-centered on their mission, adjusted their policies, and found a way to serve the community without losing themselves.

This chapter explores how churches can engage in revenue-generating activities without compromising their witness. It's not about fear. It's about faithfulness.

Theological Framing

Churches do not exist to run businesses—but they often need business-like wisdom to sustain ministry. The tension is real: how do we pursue financial responsibility without turning sacred spaces into commercial ones? How do we draw the line between what supports the mission and what distracts from it?

Paul's words in 2 Corinthians 8:21 are particularly relevant here: "For we aim at what is honorable not only in the Lord's sight but also in human sight." The early church faced its own stewardship challenges. In the context of fundraising for the Jerusalem believers, Paul insists not only on integrity before God but also transparency before others. Why? Because financial conduct is a form of testimony. It tells a story.

The same is true today. How a church handles income—whether from a rental, fundraiser, or endowment—communicates volumes. It can affirm the church's calling, or quietly erode it.

Philippians 4:8 (NIV) gives us another lens: "Finally, brothers and sisters, whatever is true, whatever is noble, whatever is right… think about such things." Revenue-generating activity, like every other form of stewardship, should be filtered through this ethic. Is it true to our purpose? Is it noble in its intent? Is it right in both process and outcome?

A congregation operating a seasonal thrift store to support mission trips found itself questioning the endeavor after several years. The shop had grown successful, but staff time was stretched, volunteers were burning out, and the financial return was no longer significant. After prayerful reflection and a mission alignment review, the board decided to close the store and redirect their focus toward direct giving campaigns and local partnerships. They mourned the loss, but celebrated the clarity.

Revenue, when rightly discerned, is not just a financial matter—it is spiritual formation in action. It trains the church to ask: What are we called to do? And what must we leave behind?

Practical Application

Revenue-generating activities come in many forms: facility rentals, thrift shops, cafés, ticketed events, vendor booths, raffles, product sales, intellectual property. The list is long—and the line between ministry and business can blur quickly.

One church began hosting yoga classes in their multipurpose room. At first, the effort was mission-aligned: it fostered wellness and brought neighbors into the space. But when they began charging for classes and marketing to the wider community, questions arose about unrelated business income tax (UBIT). The treasurer consulted with a tax professional, reviewed the church's exempt purpose, and structured the program so that it remained aligned with their health ministry. They avoided liability, clarified purpose, and strengthened the partnership.

Another church ran a café on weekday mornings. Initially volunteer-led, it began generating steady income and took on paid staff. The leadership paused to review whether the café's operation served their spiritual mission or had become an end in itself. They revised the business plan to include free community meals and reflective art exhibits, tying the café explicitly to their outreach ministry. Revenue continued—but so did the witness.

Third, a congregation launched an online marketplace to sell handmade crafts by members. While the revenue supported church programs, leaders noticed inequities: certain members gained more exposure, and the project consumed disproportionate staff energy. The treasurer worked with the board to establish a revenue policy—outlining criteria for equity, mission alignment, and compliance. Some activities were scaled back, and others restructured. Integrity improved.

Finally, one urban church rented space to a local business during weekdays to offset utility costs. When a neighbor raised concerns about zoning and signage, the church paused. They consulted their attorney and denominational office, updated their lease agreement, and added spiritual covenant language. They affirmed their welcome—without abandoning their witness.

A mid-sized suburban church with about 250 members realized they had no written contracts for several ongoing building rentals. One group had used space for years without formal terms, and another had never provided proof of insurance. After reviewing the ECLC's Revenue Generating Activities Checklist, the treasurer led a process to formalize all rental agreements, update policies, and clarify expectations. The result was increased legal protection, better scheduling, and a modest but consistent increase in revenue—all without compromising the church's hospitality.

When navigating revenue questions, wise churches ask:
- Does this activity align with our stated mission?
- Is this income subject to UBIT or other tax requirements?
- Are we tracking revenue separately and accurately?
- Could this activity create reputational or ethical confusion?
- Are we stewarding staff and volunteer energy wisely?

Churches can use a revenue tool available in church leadership communities to review existing activities, evaluate risk, and ensure policies are updated. Don't wait for a letter from the IRS to clarify your calling. Let mission lead.

Conclusion and Reflection Questions

What is right is not always what is profitable. And what is profitable is not always what is aligned with our purpose. Paul's words in 2 Corinthians 8:21 remind us that the goal is not merely compliance—it is honor. Honor before God. Honor before people. Honor in the choices we make when no one is watching. Philippians 4:8 echoes this pursuit: think on what is noble, right, admirable. The treasurer's role is not to restrict possibility, but to illuminate what is worthy.

If your church is ready to realign:
- Develop a revenue activity review plan. Inventory your income streams. Assess for mission, sustainability, and compliance.
- Host a mission-aligned fundraising workshop. Invite your board and ministry leaders into dialogue: What does faithful revenue look like here? What no longer fits?

In doing so, you'll discover that what is right—when rooted in God's purpose—is also what is most fruitful.

🌱 Reflection Questions

1. How does 2 Corinthians 8:21 (NRSVUE) inspire your role in managing revenue-generating activities as a treasurer?
2. In what ways does aligning revenue activities with mission reflect your spiritual calling?
3. How might mission-focused revenue practices strengthen your church's integrity?
4. Share a story from your experience where revenue decisions, like a church formalizing rental contracts, advanced the church's calling.
5. What steps can you take to ensure your church's revenue activities honor both God and legal standards?

Chapter 17

Keep The Faith

Succession Planning

"I have fought the good fight, I have finished the race, I have kept the faith."
— 2 Timothy 4:7 (NRSV)

Introduction

Every church will face the moment when one season of leadership ends and another begins. A beloved treasurer retires. A long-serving board chair steps away. The question is not if transition will come—but how we will prepare for it.

Succession planning is not just an administrative exercise. It is an act of hope. When Paul writes to Timothy near the end of his life, he does so with a spirit of completion and handoff: "I have fought the good fight, I have finished the race, I have kept the faith." It is a charge not only to finish well but to prepare the way for those who follow.

Hebrews 12:1 echoes this continuity: "Therefore, since we are surrounded by so great a cloud of witnesses… let us run with perseverance the race that is set before us." Church leadership is never solitary. It is a relay. And treasurers are often among the most crucial runners.

One church saw this clearly when their treasurer gave notice of retirement after 18 faithful years. Financial systems were stable, but no one else on the board knew the budget process, the payroll procedures, or the calendar of reporting obligations. The congregation was grateful—but unprepared. With prayerful discernment and guidance, the board developed a hiring and onboarding plan, shadowed the outgoing treasurer, and recruited a finance volunteer who later became their next treasurer. What could have been a crisis became a testimony to shared stewardship. Succession planning is not about filling a slot. It is about stewarding wisdom, inviting participation, and ensuring that God's work continues beyond any single leader. In this chapter, we reflect on the treasurer's role in preparing the church for transition with grace, clarity, and faith.

Theological Framing

The metaphor of a race is one of Scripture's richest for the life of faith. It conjures movement, direction, perseverance—and, importantly, a finish line. In 2 Timothy 4:7, Paul's voice is both weary and joyful: "I have fought the good fight, I have finished the race, I have kept the faith." His life has not been without struggle.

But it has been marked by faithfulness.

What makes this moment so powerful is that Paul is not clinging to his role. He is passing the baton. His letters to Timothy are full of mentorship and preparation. He does not try to do everything himself. Instead, he invests in someone else, equipping them to carry the work forward.

Succession planning, in this light, is a sacred discipline. It asks: Who will come after me? What will they need? How can I help them thrive?

Hebrews 12:1 calls us to run with perseverance "the race that is set before us," but not alone. We are surrounded by a cloud of witnesses—those who have come before and those who will come after. Good transitions honor that sacred chain.

In one congregation, a treasurer nearing retirement realized that no one had ever seen the full calendar of financial responsibilities. Reports were filed on time, payroll was smooth, but all the knowledge lived in her head. She took a sabbatical month and spent part of it writing out step-by-step guides for each core task. She met weekly with the new finance chair to review systems, answer questions, and offer prayer. When she stepped down, there was grief—but no chaos. Her preparation was a gift of peace.

Another church faced a different scenario. A sudden resignation left the board scrambling. The remaining leaders decided that such disorientation could never happen again. They created a mentorship program, pairing every officer with a second person responsible for shadowing and support. They trained board members on how to identify and raise up new leaders. Within a year, their board meetings included reflective check-ins: "What are we doing today to equip those who will lead tomorrow?"

Succession planning is not just organizational. It is spiritual. It means choosing faith over fear. It means trusting that God will continue to raise up faithful leaders if we are willing to prepare the path.

Practical Application

Succession planning is not just about finding the next treasurer—it's about preserving the integrity of the ministry through seasons of change. When churches fail to prepare, leadership transitions can leave gaps in financial knowledge, mission continuity, and trust. But with intention and prayerful foresight, transitions become opportunities for blessing.

A growing faith community found itself at such a crossroads when their long-serving treasurer gave notice of retirement after 18 faithful years. Their systems were orderly, but little had been documented. The board realized that without preparation, the next treasurer would inherit a black box. So they began a structured transition. The outgoing treasurer trained a volunteer assistant for six months, walking them through procedures, reports, and values. They also created a resource binder detailing recurring responsibilities and deadlines. When the transition came, it was not abrupt—it was a handoff filled with gratitude, celebration, and trust. The new treasurer brought fresh energy, and within a year, the church launched a new ministry initiative, building on the legacy they had inherited.

Another congregation developed a hiring and onboarding policy after struggling to recruit financial leaders. By clarifying expectations and outlining spiritual and technical qualifications, they made the treasurer role less intimidating and more attractive. The process included a 90-day onboarding window with mentoring, check-ins, and prayerful reflection. This model not only strengthened the treasurer's experience but helped the board discern and develop future leaders.

Mentorship has proven key for many churches. A medium-sized congregation established a formal mentoring process between outgoing and incoming financial leaders. The outgoing treasurer met monthly with their successor over coffee, not just to teach systems but to share the spiritual posture of the work. They prayed together, discussed challenges, and reflected on mission. This relational model created a lasting bond and laid the foundation for continued discernment.

A small urban church of about 100 members realized that most of its financial processes lived solely in the mind of their outgoing treasurer. No written procedures existed, and key calendar items were undocumented. Using the ECLC's Succession Planning Guide, the board collaborated to write down core workflows, calendar deadlines, and approval processes. They also created a transition timeline with coaching and check-ins for the incoming treasurer. The board reported smoother onboarding, greater transparency, and renewed confidence in their long-term capacity to steward resources well.

Succession isn't limited to treasurers. Churches that build leadership capacity across their boards—training members in financial language, reviewing roles annually, and rotating leadership thoughtfully—create a culture where succession is expected, not feared.

Healthy succession practices include:
- Developing clear hiring and onboarding policies that align with the church's mission and values
- Creating mentoring structures that transfer both knowledge and spiritual insight
- Preparing documentation and transition binders to support continuity
- Training board members and lay leaders to understand and steward financial systems

When succession planning is seen as an act of faith, it becomes a gift to future generations. It tells the next treasurer: "We've made a path for you. We believe in the work you'll carry forward."

Conclusion and Reflection Questions

To keep the faith is not only to run your own race well—but to ensure the next runner is ready.

The treasurer's role in succession planning is essential. It allows for wisdom to be passed, systems to be preserved, and trust to be built. It creates continuity not just in numbers, but in spirit.

Hebrews 12:1 reminds us that the church does not run alone. We are surrounded. And our legacy is shaped not only by what we've done—but by how we've equipped others to continue.

If your church is ready to prepare:

• Develop a succession planning strategy. Clarify key roles, timelines, and training phases.

• Host a leadership transition workshop. Invite stories, name gaps, and begin building a leadership culture that sees transitions as sacred.

To finish well is to begin again—for the sake of the church, and the glory of God.

🕊 Reflection Questions

1. How does 2 Timothy 4:7 (NRSV) inspire your role in fostering succession planning as a treasurer?
2. In what ways does preparing future leaders reflect your spiritual calling as a steward?
3. How might effective succession planning strengthen your church's long-term mission?
4. Share a story from your experience where succession planning, like a church documenting processes for transitions, advanced the church's calling.
5. What steps can you take to ensure your church's financial leadership transitions are seamless?

Epilogue

There's a quiet strength in those who keep the books of the church.

Not the kind that draws attention or fills a sanctuary with applause—but the kind that keeps ministry standing when storms come. The kind that makes sure the lights stay on, the payroll is met, the mission is resourced, and the community can trust what's printed in the bulletin or shared at the annual meeting. In seventeen chapters, we have journeyed through the spiritual and practical dimensions of this sacred work.

You've explored the diligence of leadership, the ethics of transparency, and the discipline of budgeting not just for sustainability but for mission. You've walked through the importance of alignment, the necessity of compliance, and the courage required to address risks, train leaders, and plan for the unknown. You've seen that financial stewardship is not about guarding resources in fear—but about releasing them with purpose.

And more than anything, you've encountered this truth: **being a treasurer is a ministry**.

One congregation I know began their turnaround when a treasurer, newly elected and barely trained, asked a single question at a board meeting: "Does our budget reflect our calling?" At first, the room fell silent. Then heads nodded. And slowly, week by week, they began to reframe their approach—not just fixing numbers, but clarifying vision. Over two years, they shifted from crisis response to mission clarity. They established a reserve policy, launched a mentoring plan for future leaders, introduced transparent financial reports, and aligned giving campaigns with spiritual values. Today, their community garden feeds dozens each week. Their financial meetings begin with prayer and end with joy. It wasn't easy. But it was holy.

That's the invitation this book extends. Not to become perfect, but to become purposeful.

In a world that continues to shift—digitally, demographically, economically—the church is being called to something deeper than survival. It is being called to stewardship that is grounded, transparent, and Spirit-led. Digital giving platforms and online financial tools are changing how we manage donations. Diverse leadership is reshaping how we define accountability. Legal and tax frameworks are evolving. But the core of this work remains unchanged: to lead with integrity, generosity, and a vision rooted in God's unfolding call.

Hebrews 12:1 reminds us: *"Since we are surrounded by so great a cloud of witnesses… let us run with perseverance the race that is set before us"* (see Appendix A). You are part of that cloud now. Each report you file, each budget you build, each conversation you guide adds to the legacy of those who came before—and clears the way for those who will come next.

So let this be your charge:

Lead with faith, not fear. The spreadsheets matter, but so does the story they tell.

Train others generously. What you know is not only for you—it is a gift to pass on.

Align your numbers with your mission. Let every dollar become a disciple, sent out to do good work.

And when the days feel long, or the questions overwhelming, remember: **you are not alone**. The same Spirit who breathed life into the early church walks beside you still—in board meetings, in stewardship campaigns, in quiet moments of prayer over a messy budget.

You have fought the good fight. You are still running the race. Keep the faith.

And may your ministry of money always be a ministry of grace.

Appendices

Introduction to Appendices

The appendices that follow are designed to support your journey as a faithful financial steward, whether you are a church treasurer, board member, or ministry leader. These practical tools complement the spiritual and actionable insights in *The Ministry of Money*, helping you apply the book's principles with clarity and confidence.

Appendix A: Scripture References lists all primary and supporting scriptures cited in the book, organized by chapter with their translations. Use this for personal study, sermon preparation, or group discussions to deepen your theological grounding.

Appendix B: Key Terms Glossary defines essential concepts, from fiduciary duty to unrelated business income tax, in accessible language. Refer to it when navigating technical terms or training new leaders.

Appendix C: Treasurer's Annual Checklist offers a concise guide to key actions for financial stewardship, from audits to succession planning. Use it to organize your responsibilities or facilitate board planning sessions.

These resources are meant to be used alongside the chapters, whether individually or in group settings like finance committee meetings or leadership workshops. May they equip you to align your church's finances with its sacred calling.

Appendix A: Scripture References

The following table lists the primary and supporting scriptures used in *The Ministry of Money: A Treasurer's Role in the Mission of the Church*, organized by chapter, with their respective translations. All scriptures are quoted in the text and referenced to this appendix, as indicated in each chapter.

Chapter	Title	Primary Scripture	Translation	Supporting Scripture	Translation
1	Called to Diligence	Romans 12:8: "if it is to lead, do it diligently; if it is to show mercy, do it cheerfully"	NIV	None specified	N/A
2	Faithful Stewards	1 Corinthians 4:2: "Now it is required that those who have been given a trust must prove faithful"	NIV	None specified	N/A
3	Guard the Deposit	2 Timothy 1:14: "Guard the good deposit entrusted to you"	NIV	None specified	N/A

Chapter	Title	Primary Scripture	Translation	Supporting Scripture	Translation
4	Prudent Leadership	Proverbs 27:12: "The prudent sees danger and takes refuge"	NIV		
5	Much Is Required	Luke 12:48: "From everyone to whom much has been given, much will be required…"	NRSV		
6	Honor the Lord	Proverbs 3:9–10: "Honor the LORD with your wealth…"	CEB		
7	Serve God Alone	Matthew 6:24: "No one can serve two masters… You cannot serve both God and wealth"	CEB		
8	Truth in the Inward Being	Psalm 51:6: "Behold, you delight in truth in the inward being…"	ESV		
9	Faithful Servants	Matthew 25:21: "Well done, good and	ESV		

Chapter	Title	Primary Scripture	Translation	Supporting Scripture	Translation
		faithful servant…"			
10	Sustaining Mission	Philippians 4:19: "And my God will supply every need of yours…"	ESV	2 Corinthians 9:8: "And God is able to make all grace abound to you…"	ESV
11	Cheerful Givers	2 Corinthians 9:7: "God loves a cheerful giver"	ESV	Psalm 90:12: "So teach us to number our days that we may get a heart of wisdom"	ESV
12	Not In Vain	Psalm 127:1: "Unless the Lord builds the house, those who build it labor in vain"	ESV	Proverbs 15:22: "Without counsel plans fail, but with many advisers they succeed"	ESV
13	Estimate The Cost	Luke 14:28: "For who among you, intending to build a tower, does not first sit down and estimate the cost, to see whether he has enough to complete it?"	NRSV	Proverbs 21:5: "The plans of the diligent lead surely to abundance…"	ESV

Chapter	Title	Primary Scripture	Translation	Supporting Scripture	Translation
14	What You Owe	Romans 13:7: "Pay to all what is due them…"	NRSVUE	Matthew 22:21: "Give back to Caesar what is Caesar's…"	NIV
15	Silence The Ignorant	1 Peter 2:13–14: "For the Lord's sake accept the authority of every human institution…"	NRSV	Titus 3:1: "Remind them to submit to rulers and authorities…"	CEB
16	What Is Right	2 Corinthians 8:21: "For we aim at what is honorable…"	NRSVUE	Philippians 4:8: "Finally, brothers and sisters, whatever is true…"	NIV
17	Keep The Faith	2 Timothy 4:7: "I have fought the good fight…"	NRSV	Hebrews 12:1: "Therefore, since we are surrounded by so great a cloud of witnesses…"	CEB

y.

Appendix B: Key Terms Glossary

This glossary defines key terms used in *The Ministry of Money: A Treasurer's Role in the Mission of the Church* to support readers new to church financial stewardship. Terms are drawn from the manuscript's content and explained in accessible language.

501(c)(3) Status: A U.S. tax-exempt designation for nonprofit organizations, including churches, allowing tax deductions for donations and exemption from certain taxes, provided they adhere to IRS regulations (e.g., avoiding political campaigning). See Chapter 14.

Bylaws: Written rules governing a church's operations, including board roles, decision-making, and membership. Regular updates ensure legal and missional alignment. See Chapter 15.

Cash Flow: The movement of money into and out of a church's accounts, reflecting income timing (e.g., pledges) and expense schedules (e.g., utilities). Managing cash flow prevents shortfalls. See Chapter 13.

Compliance: Adherence to federal, state, and local laws, such as tax filings, employment classifications, and nonprofit regulations, to maintain a church's legal standing. See Chapter 14.

Fiduciary Duty: The legal and ethical responsibility of church leaders (e.g., treasurers, board members) to act in the church's best interest, managing funds with care and transparency. See Chapters 14–15.

Governance: The systems and processes (e.g., bylaws, board meetings) guiding a church's leadership and decision-making, ensuring mission alignment and accountability. See Chapter 15.

Mission Alignment: Ensuring financial decisions (e.g., budgeting, revenue activities) reflect a church's core purpose and values, as defined by its mission statement. See Chapters 11, 16.

Stewardship: The responsible management of a church's resources (e.g., finances, facilities) as a sacred trust, reflecting faithfulness to God and the congregation. See Chapters 1–17.

Succession Planning: Preparing for leadership transitions (e.g., treasurer retirement) through hiring policies, mentorship, and training to ensure mission continuity. See Chapter 17.

Unrelated Business Income Tax (UBIT): A tax on income from activities not substantially related to a church's exempt purpose (e.g., commercial rentals), requiring careful compliance to maintain tax-exempt status. See Chapters 14, 16.

Appendix C: Treasurer's Annual Checklist

This checklist summarizes key actions for church treasurers to ensure financial stewardship, mission alignment, and compliance, drawn from *The Ministry of Money: A Treasurer's Role in the Mission of the Church*. Use annually to guide planning and reflection.

Diligence and Accountability (Chapters 1–5):

Review financial records for accuracy and transparency.

Conduct an internal audit or hire an external auditor to verify accounts.

Ensure board members understand their fiduciary duties.

Financial Management (Chapters 6–13):

Honor giving by allocating funds to mission priorities (Chapter 6).

Develop a mission-driven budget with congregational input (Chapter 11).

Create a 12-month cash flow projection to manage income/expense timing (Chapter 13).

Establish a reserve fund policy for emergencies (Chapter 10).

Compliance and Governance (Chapters 14–15):

Verify 501(c)(3) compliance, avoiding political campaigning or excessive lobbying (Chapter 14).

File IRS Form 990 (if required) and state corporate reports (Chapter 14).

Review bylaws for legal and missional alignment (Chapter 15).

Conduct board training on governance and fiduciary responsibilities (Chapter 15).

Revenue and Succession (Chapters 16–17):

Assess revenue-generating activities (e.g., rentals) for mission alignment and UBIT compliance (Chapter 16).

Develop a revenue activity review plan to ensure ethical practices (Chapter 16).

Create a succession plan for the treasurer role, including hiring and mentoring (Chapter 17).

Host a leadership transition workshop to prepare future leaders (Chapter 17).

Reflection and Renewal:

Reflect on your role as a spiritual steward using chapter reflection questions.

Pray for discernment in financial decisions, seeking God's guidance.

Index

A

Accountability

- as discipleship, 22–29, 34–41

- governance and, 138–143

- transparency in, 84–91, 98–103

Acts 4:34, 34, 167

Alignment, mission. *See* Mission alignment

Audits, 34–41, 173

- internal/external, 173

- preventing fraud, 34–41

B

Budgeting

- mission-driven, 106–113, 122–129

- transparent planning, 114–121

- cash flow in, 122–129

Bylaws, 138–143, 171, 173

C

Called Together, 10–17, 34–41, 84–91

Care, duty of, 22–29

Cash flow, 122–129, 171

- projections, 122–129, 173

Cheerful giving, 106–113

Church Training Center, i, 178

Clarity, financial, 48–55, 84–91, 114–121

Compliance, 132–137, 144–151, 171, 173

- employment regulations, 132–137

- revenue activities, 144–151

Conflict of interest, 22–29, 178

Congregations, examples

- large suburban church (400 members), 138–143

- large urban church, 114–121

- mid-sized suburban church (175 members), 22–29

- mid-sized suburban church (200 members), 98–103

- mid-sized suburban church (250 members), 144–151

- mid-sized urban church (200 members), 132–137

- small rural church (80 members), 34–41

- small urban church (100 members), 152–159

2 Corinthians 8:21, 144–151, 167

2 Corinthians 9:7, 106, 167

D

Detail, financial, 48–55

Discernment

- budget planning, 114–121, 122–129

- cash flow, 122–129

- leadership, 10–17, 84–91

- revenue activities, 144–151

Diligence, 10–17, 64–71, 173

Duty of care, 22–29

Duty of loyalty, 22–29

Duty of obedience, 22–29

E

Effective Church Leadership Community (ECLC), i, 10–17, 22–29, 34–41, 48–55, 64–71, 76–83, 84–91, 92–97, 98–103, 106–113, 114–121, 122–129, 132–137, 138–143, 144–151, 152–159, 178

- Budget Template, 178

- Compliance Checklist, 132–137

- Conflict of Interest Policy, 22–29, 178

- Financial Policies & Procedures Template, 34–41, 76–83, 92–97, 98–103, 132–137

- Governance Checklist, 138–143

- Mission Audit Template, 178

- Revenue Generating Activities Checklist, 144–151

- Succession Planning Guide, 152–159

- Trust Mapping Template, 22–29

- Whistleblower Protection Policy, 34–41

Embracing Our Call, 10–17, 22–29, 34–41, 48–55, 64–71, 76–83, 84–91, 92–97, 98–103, 106–113, 114–121, 122–129, 132–137, 138–143, 144–151, 152–159, 178

Employment regulations, 132–137

Ethics, 22–29, 84–91, 144–151

F

Faithfulness, 22–29, 48–55, 92–97, 122–129

Fiduciary duty, 22–29, 171, 173

Financial literacy, 48–55

Fraud prevention, 34–41, 178

- Sample Whistleblower Protection Policy, 34–41

G

Giving, 64–71, 106–113

- cheerful, 106–113

- transparent campaigns, 64–71

Good Governance webinar, 22–29, 34–41, 178

Governance, 138–143, 171, 173

- ECLC Governance Checklist, 138–143

H

Hebrews 12:1, 152–159, 160–166, 167

Honor, 64–71, 144–151

I

Integrity, 22–29, 34–41, 84–91, 132–137, 138–143, 144–151

- financial detail and, 48–55

L

Leadership, spiritual, 10–17, 22–29, 152–159

Loyalty, duty of, 22–29

Luke 14:28, 122–129, 167

Luke 16:10, 48–55, 167

M

Matthew 22:21, 132–137, 167

Matthew 25:21, 92–97, 167

Mentorship, 152–159

Mission alignment, 10–17, 64–71, 92–97, 98–103, 106–113, 114–121, 122–129, 132–137, 138–143, 144–151, 171

- budgeting and, 106–113, 114–121

- revenue activities and, 144–151

O

Obedience, duty of, 22–29

Oversight structures, 34–41, 98–103, 138–143, 152–159

P

1 Peter 2:13–14, 138–143, 167

Philippians 4:8, 144–151, 167

Planning

- budget, 106–113, 114–121, 122–129

- cash flow, 122–129

- succession, 152–159, 171, 173

Preventing Church Fraud webinar, 34–41, 178

Proverbs 15:22, 114–121, 167

Proverbs 21:5, 122–129, 167

Psalm 127:1, 114–121, 167

R

Reserve policy, 98–103, 160–166, 173

Revenue activities, 144–151, 171, 173

- ECLC Revenue Generating Activities Checklist, 144–151

- unrelated business income tax (UBIT), 144–151, 171

Risk management, 34–41, 178

Romans 12:8, 10–17, 167

Romans 13:7, 132–137, 167

S

Serving the Call, 10–17, 22–29, 34–41, 48–55, 84–91, 152–159, 178

Stewardship, 10–17, 22–29, 34–41, 48–55, 64–71, 76–83, 84–91, 92–97, 98–103, 106–113, 114–121, 122–129, 132–137, 138–143, 144–151, 152–159, 171

- as ministry, 10–17, 22–29, 160–166

- compliance as, 132–137

- financial detail and, 48–55

- governance and, 138–143

- revenue activities and, 144–151

Succession planning, 152–159, 171, 173

- ECLC Succession Planning Guide, 152–159

T

Transparency, 22–29, 64–71, 84–91, 98–103, 114–121, 132–137, 138–143, 173

- budget planning, 114–121

- financial reporting, 22–29, 64–71, 84–91

Trust, 22–29, 34–41, 64–71, 84–91, 98–103, 114–121, 138–143, 152–159

- building, 22–29, 64–71, 84–91

- ECLC Trust Mapping Template, 22–29

2 Timothy 1:14, 34–41, 167

2 Timothy 4:7, 152–159, 167

U

Unrelated business income tax (UBIT), 144–151, 171

W

Whistleblower protection, 34–41

Effective Church Leadership Community

The Effective Church Leadership Community (ECLC) offers a wealth of tools and training to support church leaders in their mission-driven roles. The following resources are curated to enhance your effectiveness as a treasurer or board member, providing foundational guidance for governance, spiritual alignment, strategic planning, and financial stewardship. Access these resources through the ECLC at

Scan the QR code below or visit:
https://community.churchtrainingcenter.com/plans/1538011

where you'll find webinars, downloadable templates, and foundational texts to deepen your leadership journey.

Top Webinars in the Effective Church Leadership Community

These five webinars offer essential training for church treasurers, board members, and clergy. Each one equips leaders to make faithful, mission-aligned financial decisions and strengthen church governance.

Good Governance
Learn the core duties of church boards—care, loyalty, and obedience—along with practical steps for ethical, effective leadership.

Church Board Meetings Focused on God's Calling
Discover how to lead spiritually grounded meetings that align decisions with your church's purpose and values.

Developing an Effective Church Strategic Plan
Gain tools to build a mission-driven plan that integrates vision, finances, and long-term ministry goals.

Risk Management for Church Leadership
Explore proactive strategies to reduce legal, financial, and reputational risks within your church.

Preventing Church Fraud
Understand common fraud risks and learn practical systems to safeguard your church's finances and build trust.

Top Downloadable Resources in the ECLC

These ready-to-use tools help treasurers and board members implement best practices in financial management, ethical leadership, and mission alignment.

New Church Board Member Orientation Checklist
A step-by-step guide to onboard new board members and treasurers with confidence and clarity.

Sample Church Covenant of Behavior
A customizable agreement to foster respectful, mission-centered leadership and healthy board culture.

Sample Conflict of Interest Policy
A clear, practical policy to ensure transparency, accountability, and ethical decision-making.

Mission Audit Template
A reflective tool to evaluate how church activities align with its core calling and spiritual priorities.

Budget Template
An easy-to-use format for developing clear, transparent, and mission-aligned church budgets.

Continue the Journey

These additional resources from Church Training Center are designed to support your journey as a faithful financial leader. Each tool offers deeper guidance for different parts of the path—from governance and planning to hands-on stewardship and formation.

To learn more or access these resources, visit
https://churchtrainingcenter.com/publications/

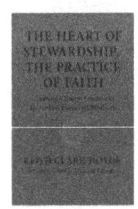

The Heart of Stewardship, The Practice of Faith

This workbook accompanies The Ministry of Money and provides practical, spiritual exercises for local church treasurers. It reinforces spiritual calling and financial clarity through hands-on practice, reflection prompts, and technical application.

Embracing Our Call: A Practical Guide for Church Governing Body Leaders

This practical guidebook equips church governing body leaders to lead with spiritual clarity, legal integrity, and faithful discernment. Grounded in Spirit-led governance, it offers biblical insight, real-life application, and reflection questions to align your board's work with God's Calling.

Serving the Call: A Training Manual for New Governance Body Members

This workbook accompanies *Embracing Our Call* and provides training for new members of church governing bodies. With templates, checklists, and facilitation tools, it offers step-by-step guidance to support faithful leadership, spiritual alignment, and board effectiveness from day one.

Called Together: A Spirit-Led Discernment Guide for Congregational Planning

This Spirit-led planning guide helps congregations discern God's vision for their shared future. Through reflective exercises, seasonal rhythms, and collaborative discernment tools, it invites churches to listen deeply, clarify their Calling, and move forward with unity and purpose.